Praise for *Somewhere in France*

"Schaeper presents an intimate look at New York doughboy, Frederick A. Kittleman. Throughout the book, Schaeper offers the appropriate context while allowing Kittleman's voice the lead during his training, travel overseas, combat experience, and postwar activities. Kittleman's faith and family fortified him with the strength necessary to endure and survive the Western Front—a century later, it would behoove us to learn from Kittleman's character. Schaeper provides us with a superb representation of the doughboy."

— Edward A. Gutiérrez, author of *Doughboys on the Great War: How American Soldiers Viewed Their Military Experience*

"Located in the space where personal and national history intersect, *Somewhere in France* places us with Frederick Kittleman in training camp and on the front lines in ways battle histories seldom do. Routine details of Sunday menus and army inoculations come alive through Frederick's entertaining voice, preserving a historical moment which shaped the twentieth century. Schaeper's skillful editing creates a cohesive narrative linked by his own informative and engaging comments. Kudos to Schaeper for recognizing the value of this fascinating look into the life of an ordinary soldier. I couldn't put it down."

— Celia M. Kingsbury, author of *For Home and Country: World War I Propaganda on the Home Front*

Somewhere in France

Somewhere in France

The World War I Letters and Journal of
Private Frederick A. Kittleman

THOMAS J. SCHAEPER

excelsior editions

State University of New York Press
Albany, New York

Cover image of Fred "Over There." Courtesy of Robert Deckman.

Published by State University of New York Press, Albany

Excelsior Editions is an imprint of State University of New York Press

For information, contact State University of New York Press, Albany, NY
www.sunypress.edu

Production, Diane Ganeles
Marketing, Fran Keneston

Library of Congress Cataloging-in-Publication Data

Names: Kittleman, Frederick A., 1896–1976, author. | Schaeper, Thomas J., author.
Title: Somewhere in France : the World War I letters and journal of Private Frederick A. Kittleman / Thomas J. Schaeper.
Description: Albany, NY : State University of New York Press, 2017. | Series: Excelsior editions | Includes bibliographical references and index.
Identifiers: LCCN 2016031435 (print) | LCCN 2016031762 (ebook) | ISBN 9781438463766 (pbk. : alk. paper) | ISBN 9781438463773 (e-book)
Subjects: LCSH: Kittleman, Frederick A., 1896–1976—Correspondence. | World War, 1914–1918—Personal narratives, American. | United States. Army. Field Artillery, 304th. | Soldiers—United States—Correspondence. | Olean (N.Y.)—Biography.
Classification: LCC D570.9.K59 2017 (print) | LCC D570.9 (ebook) | DDC 940.4/1273092 [B] —dc23
LC record available at https://lccn.loc.gov/2016031435

10 9 8 7 6 5 4 3 2 1

Contents

List of Illustrations / vii

Acknowledgments / ix

Introduction / xi

Editorial Note / xxiii

The Letters / 1

Epilogue: The Return to Civilian Life / 119

Notes / 131

Suggested Readings / 135

Index / 139

Illustrations

Figure 1. New Recruits at Camp Upton   2

Figure 2. The Feared Needle   14

Figure 3. USS *Leviathan*   27

Figure 4. French 75mm Field Gun   29

Figure 5. Letter of May 9, 1918   31

Figure 6. In Training at Camp de Souge   33

Figure 7. Louie Nobles, Little French Maiden, and Fred   44

Figure 8. Fred "Over There"   49

Figure 9. Map: Areas of 77th Division's Activity   51

Figure 10. French 75s at the Start of the Meuse-Argonne
           Drive   67

Figure 11. Doughboys Ready to Advance   70

Figure 12. Rain and Mud   75

Figure 13. Tired, Dirty, Ragged, and Lousy   79

Figure 14. James McManus and Fred   86

Figure 15. The Medieval Pageant   97

Figure 16. French 40-Man Freight Car   99

Figure 17. Fred's Sister Helen   104

Figure 18. Fred's Brother Harry   106

Figure 19. French Government Citation   110

Figure 20. Fred's Bugle   114

Figure 21. Returning Troops on USS *Agamemnon*   116

Figure 22. Fred's Mother Josephine, Fred, and Daughter Rita   127

Figure 23. Lucinda and Fred   128

Acknowledgments

After a lapse of many years, I resumed work on this project in 2013 and hoped that there were still people in Fred Kittleman's hometown who remembered him. I knew that he had died in 1976, and so I placed an ad in the local paper, the *Olean Times Herald*. To my great joy I received several phone calls from his relatives and friends. First and foremost, I must thank Robert Deckman, son of Kittleman's daughter Helen. Deckman knew his "gramps" intimately. During fishing trips Fred told him many stories. After his grandfather's death, Deckman inherited a large stack of papers and photographs. Displaying great trust in me and in the United States Postal Service, he sent me all of these materials from his home in Arizona. Other persons who shared reminiscences and photos with me include Fred's niece Lois Zach, his nephew Donald Wenke, and his granddaughter Beverly Hollander.

Numerous other persons also have helped me. My student Chris Domes did initial research on this topic and demonstrated that Fred Kittleman's story was both doable and worthwhile. Two other students aided me once I took up this project. Leah Brownstein transcribed many of the letters and helped with research. In the final stages of my work, Shannon Conheady did proofreading and solved some computer issues that befuddled my aging pate. My colleague Maddalena Marinari read the entire manuscript and offered many valuable suggestions. Members of the staff in Friedsam Memorial Library proved immensely helpful. These included archivist Dennis Frank, who carefully preserves the Kittleman letters and other World War I manuscripts; Theresa Shaffer, who manages to obtain even the most obscure interlibrary loan materials; Mary Jane Wepasnick, who aided me in locating old copies of area newspapers. Bernard Vossler, the director of the St. Bonaventure Cemetery, was able to find burial dates for numerous persons in the Kittleman, Edel, and other families. With those dates I was then able to find published obituaries and related materials. In addition, Dean David Danahar and Provost Joseph Zimmer provided essential funding that helped bring this project to fruition.

I obtained many of the details regarding the Kittleman family from records in the Olean Point Museum. Aiding me there were Dave Deckman, Olean's City Historian, and Louise Koenig, office manager of the Olean Historical and Preservation Society. I also relied heavily on articles printed in the *Olean Evening Herald*, the *Olean Morning Times*, and the *Olean Evening Times*. Those papers merged in 1932 to become the *Olean Times Herald*.

Finally, I am greatly indebted to everyone with whom I worked at SUNY Press. I benefitted from their courtesy and professionalism at every stage of the publishing process. Moreover, the anonymous readers who reviewed the manuscript for the press obviously were experts in the field, for they provided numerous valuable suggestions for improving this book.

Introduction

My acquaintance with Frederick A. Kittleman commenced in 1983. In that year a man entered Friedsam Memorial Library at St. Bonaventure University and placed a box of papers on the circulation desk. He said he lived in nearby Olean, New York. He was about to move out of town and had been cleaning his attic. There he discovered a stack of papers that he had never previously noticed. Upon glancing at them, he could see that they were letters dealing with World War I. Rather than toss them out, he thought that he should donate them to a library. Before the student who was working at the circulation desk could get the name of the stranger, he left the library. To this day we do not know who he was or where he was living when he found the letters.

Shortly after this, the letters were deposited in the library's archives. I was (and still am) a professor of history at the university. The library's staff alerted me to the collection. I glanced through the several dozen letters and found them fascinating. They are a nearly complete set of the letters that an Olean man, Frederick A. Kittleman, wrote to his family from the time of his departure for the Army in February 1918 until his arrival back home in May 1919. I thought they would make a superb research project for an undergraduate. In 1985 one of my students, Christopher Domes, transcribed and edited a large portion of the letters. He did a marvelous job in deciphering Kittleman's handwriting and in finding some details about Kittleman's life from before and after the war. In the years since 1985, I have thought often of the Kittleman letters. There was much more to be done with them. But competing research projects always seemed to pull me in other directions. Finally, as the world approached the centennial of the brutal war that erupted in 1914, I thought that the time had arrived to do full justice to these letters.

To understand Fred Kittleman's role in the war, one must first know the general background. On June 28, 1914, Archduke Franz Ferdinand and his wife were assassinated in Sarajevo, the capital of the Austro-Hungarian provinces of Bosnia and Herzegovina. Franz Ferdinand was the nephew of Emperor Franz Josef of Austria-Hungary and heir to that throne. The assassin was Gavrilo Princip, a member of a secret terrorist group called the Black Hand. The Black Hand was secretly supported by neighboring Serbia, which hoped to expand and control as much of the Balkans as possible.

With the seemingly infallible benefit of hindsight, it is easy for us today to look at the events of the next few weeks and conclude that a world war was inevitable. Few at the time would have thought so. The aging Franz Josef had not even liked his nephew and expressed no great sorrow upon learning of his death. Several of the other major powers in Europe were more concerned at that moment with their own domestic issues. Great Britain, for example, was coping with the potentially explosive decision to grant home rule to Ireland. The French press was more concerned with a lurid murder trial involving marital infidelity and charges of political corruption among high government officials. One historian has described the general diplomatic situation this way:

In the early summer of 1914, Europe was happily at peace. No country openly claimed another's territory. Kaiser

Wilhelm II of Germany and Czar Nicholas II of Russia had been on yachting holidays together. Ties between Germany and Britain were particularly close: Wilhelm had been at the deathbed of his grandmother Queen Victoria; more than 50,000 Germans were working in London or other British cities; and Germany was Britain's largest trading partner. In late June, British cruisers and battleships visited Germany's annual Elbe Regatta, where the Kaiser donned his uniform as an honorary British admiral. When the Royal Navy warships sailed for home, their commander sent a signal to his German counterpart: FRIENDS IN PAST AND FRIENDS FOREVER.[1]

Nonetheless, by early August, the most powerful nations in Europe were at war against each other in two powerful blocs: Britain, France, and Russia versus Germany and Austria-Hungary. How had this come about? Part of the explanation was a series of entangling defensive alliances. The result was that if one country went to war, its allies were expected to follow. Britain, France, and Russia were loosely tied together in what came to be called the Triple Entente. Once the war started they were generally referred to as the Allies. Germany, Austria-Hungary, and Italy formed the Triple Alliance. (When war erupted, Italy opted to stay neutral. With promises from Britain and France of territorial gains, Italy joined the Allies in 1915). Because Germany and Austria-Hungary were caught in the middle between Britain and France in the west and Russia in the east, they came to be called the Central Powers.

These alliances, however, form only part of the explanation for the outbreak of hostilities. Most scholars today agree that, in the end, each nation concluded that war was in its national interest. The belief that such a war would be a short one made such a decision easier to make. The question of which country was most guilty of causing the war is one that continues to spark debate today. Some scholars point an accusatory finger at Germany and Austria-Hungary; others look more to actions of France and Russia; yet others conclude that all the major powers share in the blame. Austria-Hungary aggressively pressured Serbia to reveal its complicity in the assassination, while Germany gave full backing to Vienna. Russia felt compelled to support its Slavic brethren in Serbia, and it did so with support from its French ally. Still smarting from its defeat in the Franco-Prussian war of 1870–1871, France wanted to achieve revenge against Germany and regain some of its lost honor. During the weeks following the assassination, some doubted whether Britain would honor its commitment to aid France and Russia. Many scholars have maintained that Germany and Austria-Hungary would have been more conciliatory toward Serbia if the British government had made it clear that it would enter the fight.

All the major powers were consumed by imperial rivalries and the militant spirit of nationalism that reigned in that era. When the European powers went to war, their colonial empires joined them. Britain had the largest empire in the history of the world, and tens of thousands of Canadians, Australians, New Zealanders, Indians, and others, would die fighting for the Union Jack. Additional nations were enticed with promises of territorial or economic gains to join the fray. Hence, Japan, Portugal, Greece, Romania, and some Latin American countries joined the Allies, while the Ottoman Empire and Bulgaria joined the Central Powers.[2]

What is beyond dispute is that no one expected the bloodbath that would consume the next four years. Most national leaders thought that this dispute would "clear the air" and be settled before Christmas. What they failed to consider was that, for the first time in history, countries would, thanks to the Industrial Revolution, be able to produce deadly weapons on an unprecedented scale. Tanks, airplanes, machine guns, flame throwers, and poison gas would make a mockery of any belief in gentlemanly warfare.

Germany's initial strategy was called the Schlieffen Plan. In it Germany hoped to make a quick foray through neutral Belgium into northern France, knock out any Allied resistance, and then send most of its troops eastward to vanquish the Russians. But that did not happen. German war planners had not counted on large numbers of British troops arriving in France just weeks after the declaration of war. The combined British and French forces managed to stop the Germans in September, some 40 miles from Paris, in what came to be called the first Battle of the Marne. In the stalemate that resulted, both sides began to dig trenches. By the end of 1914 there were trenches extending almost 500 miles from the North Sea in Belgium through northern France to the border of neutral Switzerland. Actually, there were about 25,000 miles of trenches, as each side had numerous intersecting lines. From the air they would have resembled a huge, complex spider web. Over the next four years, when one side or the other attempted to break through the enemy's lines, barbed wire entangled and machine guns mowed down the infantry troops ordered to go "over the top." The result was that the opposing lines of trenches moved very little. And because Germany had failed to knock Britain and France out of the war, it did not have enough troops to achieve a quick victory in Russia. Ineptitude and disarray at every level in the Russian government and army caused the war there to drag on as it did in the West.[3]

In the summer of 1914 few Americans would have guessed that their country eventually would join the conflict. When news of Sarajevo reached the White House at the end of June, President Woodrow Wilson paid more attention to the declining health of his wife Ellen, who would die in August, than he did to telegrams concerning events in Eastern Europe. A few weeks after hostilities commenced, he issued a formal proclamation of neutrality, urging citizens to be impartial in thought as well as in action. A North Dakota newspaper, the *Grand Forks Journal*, pretty much reflected the attitude of many Americans when it concluded, "To the world, or to a nation, an archduke more or less makes little difference."[4] For the first two and a half years of the war, the official position of the United States was neutrality. This country had become an international economic giant, but diplomatically it still clung to an isolationist tradition that had begun with George Washington's admonitions against any foreign entanglements. Most Americans tended to be more sympathetic to the Allied cause, but the vast majority agreed that this war was not theirs. The war divided the nation, because joining it would mean that recent immigrants might have to fight against people in the countries from which they had come.

Both the Allies and the Central Powers violated the neutral rights of American commercial shipping. According to the traditions of international law, a neutral power could trade with belligerent nations, provided that it was not selling military supplies of any kind. Both Britain and Germany wanted to stop the United States from trading with the other side. Britain, however, possessed the largest navy in the world. British warships occasionally intercepted American merchant ships and prevented them from traveling to German ports in the Baltic. The American government protested but achieved little response from Britain. At least no American ships or lives were lost due to British actions. The German navy was much inferior to that of Britain, and most of its surface ships remained bottled up in ports throughout the war. German submarines, however, were able to escape British patrols and cruise through the Atlantic. Unlike a British warship, a relatively small German submarine could not come to the surface and intimidate a much larger, armed merchant ship. As a result, the only method the Germans had to prevent Americans or anyone else from trading with Britain was to sink the vessels, thereby causing the loss of ships, cargoes, and lives. Germany also placed mines in many waters around the British Isles in an effort to destroy any incoming or outgoing ships. No American merchant ships were targeted in the early years of the war, but in an eight-month period in 1915 German U-boats sank 580 French and British merchant ships, many of them carrying food and other materials from the United States. It was in this period that the loss of one ship in particular caused a huge uproar in America. This was the torpedoing of the British ocean liner RMS *Lusitania* near the Irish coast in May 1915. The ship had been sailing from New York to Liverpool. Germany had declared that the waters surrounding the British Isles were a war zone, and newspaper ads in some 50 American newspapers had warned Americans of the danger in traveling on British ships. The *Lusitania* was no mere passenger liner, as it carried vast stores of war materials for British use. Altogether, 1,198 lives were lost, including those of 128 Americans. President Wilson bitterly condemned this action, and the British made good use of the sinking of the *Lusitania* in heating up anti-German sentiment in the United States. Wilson warned the Germans that if they persisted in such atrocities the United States would have to respond with force. The German government apologized and eventually halted its U-boat attacks.[5]

By early 1917, however, Germany realized that it had no choice but to resume submarine warfare. Kaiser Wilhelm II's government hoped that it would be able to choke the British economy and bring an end to the conflict before the United States could mobilize a large number of troops and transport them to Europe. (By the end of the war U-boats had sunk some 5,000 merchant vessels.) The sinking of American ships in February and March of 1917 came on the heels of the discovery in January of the notorious Zimmermann telegram, named after the German foreign minister. In that telegram, Germany tried to entice Mexico to join it in the war, with promises to aid Mexico in regaining parts of Texas, New Mexico, and Arizona. On April 6, 1917, the United States officially declared war on the Central Powers.[6]

It proved to be impossible for the United States to make a big contribution to the war effort immediately. Its armed forces were relatively modest in size. At the start of 1917, the U.S. Army consisted of fewer than 200,000 men—about 128,000 in the Regular Army and 67,000 or so in National Guard units scattered throughout the states. This combined force ranked 17th in the world in terms of size, and significantly below that in terms of training, experience, and equipment. In the spring of 1917 few in government realized just how many men the armed forces would need. President Wilson appointed General John J. "Black Jack" Pershing to command the U.S. Army in Europe, and after months of careful analysis the latter estimated that the Army would eventually need up to four million men. (The United States expected the fighting to extend into 1919. When the armistice was signed in November 1918 the Army had grown to nearly four million men, with more than half of them already in France.) The mass of new recruits would make up what came to be called the National Army—as opposed to the seasoned troops who already served in the Regular Army. To create this huge force, in May Congress passed the Selective Service Program, that is, the draft. Beginning on June 5, 1917, every man in the country between the ages of 21 and 30 was required to register with his local board. For the rest of that year and most of 1918, local draft boards called up men in successive lotteries, with each locality being expected to meet a particular quota.

One of the men who registered in June was Frederick Albert Kittleman of Olean, New York. He had been born on February 20,

1896, and since 1912 he had worked as a machinist in the local yard of the Pennsylvania Railroad. He was accompanied to the draft board by his 19-year-old bother Harry. The latter had obtained a diploma from Olean's Westbrook Commercial Academy and was working as a clerk in the Olean Trust Company.[7] Because of his age, Harry was deemed too young for the draft. Fred and Harry were the children of Frederick Alfred Kittleman and his wife Josephine. There was also a younger sister in the family, Helen, born in 1904. By 1917 the father and mother had been separated for some time. Being good Catholics, they never divorced. As will be seen in the letters below, the father was a rather remote figure by 1917. He continued to live somewhere nearby, working as a night watchman in a local brewery, but he had few contacts with the family. The father's absence had caused young Fred to quit high school before graduation and take a job at the railroad.

Fred, Harry, and Helen lived with their mother in a modest house located at 1115 West Sullivan Street. The city of Olean, 75 miles southeast of Buffalo in western New York State, was a prosperous market town and railroad hub of about 16,000 residents, bustling with factories, and surrounded by thriving dairy farms, forests rich in timber, and hills filled with productive oil wells. The factories included tanneries plus establishments specializing in steel fabrication. The first discovery of oil in North America had occurred in the nearby town of Cuba in 1627. The Olean area and nearby northwestern Pennsylvania together formed the largest high-grade oil producing center in the world in the late nineteenth and early twentieth centuries. Olean was also the starting point of the world's first major oil pipeline. It was commissioned in 1881 by John D. Rockefeller and extended 315 miles from Olean to Bayonne, New Jersey. The pipeline operated until 1927. The city was also important for the manufacture of compressors and drilling engines used in the petroleum industry. Only in the

1930s did oil production in places like Texas and Oklahoma begin to eclipse the Olean area.

Sometime in the fall of 1917 Fred Kittleman's name was selected in a new pool of local recruits. He reported to the nearby board, where he passed a physical exam and answered a series of questions about his interests and skills. He was approved for military service. The date for departure was set at February 27, 1918. Kittleman was to travel with 63 other men from Olean and surrounding towns. The night before they left home, local businessmen treated them to a banquet at the local Knights of Columbus hall. The following evening a grand parade of townspeople escorted Kittleman and the others to the Erie Railroad depot. At midnight the new draftees boarded a train that would deliver them late the following evening to a training camp on Long Island.[8]

The letters that make up the bulk of this book were written by Kittleman from the time he left home until he was about to return to America in the spring of 1919. All of the letters to his mother, brother, and sister were sent to their home on West Sullivan Street. In a couple of letters he refers to other letters that he wrote to them, but those are now missing. Either his family misplaced them or, given the vagaries of mail service in wartime, the letters never reached them. None of the letters that they wrote to him have survived, for understandable reasons. Kittleman would have had no way to carry with him all of the missives he received from family and friends. It is clear from his letters that he also wrote frequently to a large number of relatives and neighbors. His mother had two sisters and six brothers, and writing to just those people alone would have kept Kittleman busy. As far as can be determined, the letters he wrote to all of these other people no longer exist.

At the outset, one should make clear what one should not expect from these letters. They do not give a general picture of American strategy or tactics. Like enlisted men in every army in every century, Kittleman knew little about what was happening in the broad scheme of things. Often he did not know where he was going until he arrived there, and even then he sometimes had only a vague idea where he was. Moreover, once he departed training camp and headed across the Atlantic all of his letters were censored. One of the officers in his unit read and initialed everything he wrote. He was not allowed to name his location or give any specifics that might help the enemy, in case the letters were intercepted. If a reader wants to know more precisely what the U.S. Army in France was doing on any given day, there are many excellent publications that provide such information. The suggested readings at the end of this book mention some of these works.

So what do Kittleman's letters tell us? First and foremost, they give us an intimate look at what the war meant to an ordinary private. Even without being permitted to mention very many specifics, Kittleman was able to convey the unquestioning patriotism of most of the common soldiers of that era. His letters also show how the war changed him, as he went from being eager to "get a crack" at the Germans to having seen "all the action any sane man could want." The pages that follow will also allow the reader to compare what Kittleman wrote to his family to the events he chose not to write about. Not wanting to frighten his mother and siblings, he omitted mention of some of the things that happened to him. Several surviving documents enable us to see some of the horrors that he kept to himself.

In addition, these letters give us a remarkable glimpse of what many families and small towns were like a century ago. One sees the unabashed expressions of love that a man of that time could have for his siblings. How many young men today would consider writing a letter (or e-mail or text message) to their younger sisters calling them a "dear little bunch of orange blossoms"? Or would a man today be likely to write to his brother "with loads of love." The letters make clear that Kittleman lived in a tight-knit community where everyone knew and cared for his neighbors. In reading his letters one might be reminded of a sentimental old Frank Capra movie, perhaps one like *It's a Wonderful Life* with James Stewart. To be sure, there were many bad things about "the good old days." Olean, like all cities at that time, had innumerable household chimneys and factory smokestacks belching unfiltered black coal fumes into the atmosphere; and Olean still had a long way to go in areas like women's liberation and racial justice. Nonetheless, Kittleman's letters reveal many of the positive aspects of community life that have almost disappeared a century later.

Finally, these letters paint a vivid portrait of a common man, one who did not rise to become an army general or a captain of industry. But Fred Kittleman clearly was honest, thoughtful, funny, and brave. In short, someone well worth remembering.

Editorial Note

In all the letters that follow, Kittleman's spelling and punctuation have been left as he wrote them. Parentheses appear where Kittleman himself used them to insert words into his text. Brackets are used wherever I have added a word or explanation. Finally, asterisks indicate notes that I have added at the end of a letter. One must bear in mind that Kittleman usually was writing in haste, often in poor light, after a day of marching or fighting, and without the benefit of a computer's spell checker.

He was assigned to the 304th Field Artillery. For details on that regiment's location or activity on any given day, I have relied heavily on the official regimental history. Entitled *The Autobiography of a Regiment: A History of the 304th Field Artillery in the World War*, it was written by the regimental chaplain, James M. Howard, and privately printed in New York in 1920. That book contains many humorous ink drawings done by the men of the 304th, and several of these are included in the pages below. The 304th Field Artillery was part of the 77th Division. The latter's movements are chronicled in the American Battle Monuments Commission's volume *77th Division: Summary of Operations in the World War*, Washington, DC: U.S. Government Printing Office, 1944.

Throughout his time in the army, Kittleman kept on his person a notebook in which he jotted down names, addresses, and occasional remarks about his daily activities. This notebook and some other materials now belong to his grandson, Robert Deckman. I will call the notebook his journal. When I cite other materials from this collection, I will refer to them as coming from the Deckman papers.

In working on this project I have come to feel as if I knew Fred Kittleman personally. I hope that the reader will share this sense of intimacy. Because of this I will refer to him simply as Fred from this point on.

The Letters

The following brief note was Fred's first communication with his family. He had been away from home just a few hours when he hurriedly scribbled a couple of lines on a postcard. The postmark shows that it was mailed from Sterlington, New York, on February 28, 1918. When the train taking him from Olean stopped briefly at the station there, he must have run out to deposit the card in a mailbox.

Still on are way to Camp it is now 12:30 and we are still 45 min away feeling like a king dont worry.

My regards to all
Fred

♦ ♦ ♦

Fred's destination was Camp Upton, located in Yaphank, about 60 miles east of New York City on Long Island. Upton was one of several dozen new training camps that were hastily built in the months after the United States entered the war. The U.S. Army would expand to nearly twenty times its pre-war size by the end of 1918. The site of Camp Upton had been a dense, muddy forest in the summer of 1917. Thousands of civilian and army workmen had transformed it into a huge training facility by the time Fred arrived there. The camp could hold more than 40,000 soldiers at a time. During Fred's weeks there, most of the soldiers belonged to the 77th Division, which included the regiment to which Fred was assigned. The camp was so large that many new recruits got lost while trying to find their way around.

The most famous soldier in the camp was Irving Berlin, who had already become a wealthy legend for his ragtime songs and Broadway shows. The 29-year-old Berlin had been drafted in 1917. The army did not want him to fight, but rather to compose patriotic songs. While at Upton in 1918, Berlin wrote a popular musical revue entitled "Yip Yip Yaphank." The revue's most popular song was "Oh! How I Hate to Get Up in the Morning." One of its stanzas goes as follows:

> Someday I'm going to murder the bugler,
> Someday they're going to find him dead;
> I'll amputate his reveille
> And step upon it heavily,
> And spend the rest of my life in bed.

Fred obviously realized that Berlin was joking. As will be seen further below, he chose to become a bugler.

FIGURE 1. New recruits being mustered at Camp Upton (Author's Collection).

◆ ◆ ◆

Camp Upton
2-28-1918 9:00 pm

Dearest Mother, sister and brother,
　　I haven't much time to write a very long letter at this time as
it is bed time. We did not arrive into Camp Upton until pretty near
6:00 pm, then we had to stand around until they could find acco-
madations for us. We then proceeded to the Mess hall, and our feed
tasted pretty good to us because we were all tired out and hungry,
the only thing that they served us on the train was three sandwiches
a couple of fried eggs and a cup of coffee. For supper we had Boiled
beef, mashed potatoes, gravey and canned corn, cocoa, lard bread, the
only thing seemed very funny for me was the fact that there was'nt
any butter on the table.
　　After supper our company went out to the toilet and washed
up. (We ate supper without even cleaning up)
　　The next thing in order, said company, had to report to the commanding officer and answer to roll call, also to get an identification
card, as we are liable to get lost in the camp. Mother you dont and
can't even realize how large this camp is, some of the fellows said it
was about 15 miles square. —March 1, We had to get up at 5:45 am
this morning, something new for me eh what? After breakfast, which
consisted of Oat meal, hass [hash?], bread and coffee we had to go
out on the parade grounds and drill for about one hr. After that we
marched to the Medical Examiners, and got examined, vaccinated,
and got a shot in the arm
　　They sent us back to barracks to rest, so I [am] finishing letter
I started last night, so I am patiantly waiting for dinner. They said
we would get our uniforms today so I'll probably will be sending my
clothes, and a little bit more of that super baggage I took along.

Letters / 3

All the boy's, including myself, are well and contented with this life, as far as it has gone. There were 574 men on the train that brought us from Olean, Ger, but it was tiresome trip, beleive me.

Now mother and sister I want to pour forth a little praise for you, on my leaving home, you done yourself a big credit. Now I dont want you to worry about me at all, because as soon as I get a furlough I will come home.

Mother there is some things that I want, and that is a few one cent stamps and one good pencil. Harry told me that you didn't need another stamp on those post cards, but I found out and they said I did. The Engineer corp down here is going over [to France] next week, so I wont try to get in that until they form a new division. Now dont worry and fret about me because I am in a good company, and will take good care of myself. The watch Harry gave I can't regulate at all, I will try again to day and if she is not alright will send it back.

Give all the neighbours my best and tell them I will write later.

With love to all,
Fred.

My temporary address is

Casual Barracks*
Btry F 304th F.A.
Camp Upton

P.S. Am sending a few views of Camp Upton. Tell me if you have heard from Aunt Frieda.

---

*"Casual" refers to men who have not yet been given assignments. In this case, Fred was temporarily in barracks for men who had not yet been housed with their units.

♦ ♦ ♦

Fred's brother Harry, born in 1898, was exempted from the draft for two reasons: he was under the age of 21, and after Fred departed he was the sole breadwinner supporting the family. By the time of this letter, Harry had taken a job with Fred's former employer, the Pennsylvania Railroad.

♦ ♦ ♦

3-2-18

Dear Brother,

This certainly has been one busy day for yours truly up at Revellee, which is at 5:45 breakfast at 7:00 drill from 8:00 until 11:30 dinner drill at 1:00 until 5:00pm then supper, the rest of the time I will spend in writing. God, is awful to have so many friends. Well Harry I suppose this card will bore the life out of you but I have got to fill it up. Harry this is a pretty good life for a young boy like myself.

Will write a letter later, so don't fret.

♦ ♦ ♦

Below Fred reports that he chose Field Artillery as his branch of service, because, he says, it is easiest. That was only partly true. The doughboys in the infantry suffered the highest mortality rates, but all the men risked death or injury. During active fighting, those in the field artillery generally were situated a few thousand yards behind the infantry regiments. The job of the artillery was to bombard the enemy with hours of shelling prior to an infantry attack. Once the infantry began to move, the artillery kept up its firing on the enemy. But just as American artillery could hurl shells well into enemy lines, so too enemy artillery could fire shells or gas canisters at American artillery emplacements. Here and in later letters Fred does his best to conceal from his family the real dangers that he faced.

Of the four million draftees and volunteers in the Army by the end of 1918, two million served in France in the American Expeditionary Force (AEF). The war ended before the other two million could be processed and shipped across the ocean. Fred and the great majority of the soldiers at Camp Upton during his time there were part of the 77th Division. This division was one of the first army divisions composed primarily of draftees. The 77th consisted of approximately 30,000 troops—the number varied, as many officers and men were constantly being transferred in or out. Most of the men in this division came from the greater New York City area, and thus the 77th came to be called variously "New York's Own" as well as the "Statue of Liberty Division," the "Metropolitan Division," and the "Empire State Division." Thousands of the 77th's new recruits were immigrants who spoke no English. Thus, in addition to learning how to be soldiers, they had to learn the language. Fred belonged to contingents arriving from Olean, Buffalo, and other cities in western New York. By the spring of 1918, the 77th also included a smattering of recruits from the Midwest. A Major General commanded the division. The 77th was divided into three brigades—two of infantry and one of field artillery. The field artillery brigade contained three artillery regiments plus three machine gun battalions, an engineer regiment, a field signal battalion, and several other units. The regiment to which Fred was assigned was the 304th Field Artillery, which was commanded by a Colonel or Lieutenant Colonel. The 304th was divided into two battalions, each under a Major. The second battalion consisted of Batteries D, E, and F. The last one would be Fred's "home" for the duration of the war. Battery F had about 200 men in it at any given time. It was usually led by a Captain and two Lieutenants. Howard's regimental history lists twelve other Olean men, most of them Fred's friends, in this same battery.

Fred's conviction that he was fighting for an honorable cause can be seen throughout his letters. In this he reflected the sentiments of the great majority of Americans. Already by 1915 sentiment across the country had slowly been turning in favor of Britain and its allies.[1] While not being jingoistic, the Olean newspapers from 1917 to 1919 wholeheartedly supported the cause and reported on all the Olean men who went "over there." Repeatedly, the people from Fred's hometown oversubscribed the liberty bond drives that were held periodically to provide the government with funds for the military. Olean's mayor, Foster Studholme, declared that all able-bodied men must "Either work, fight, or go to jail. . . . There is work enough for all and to go around. . . . I have instructed the local police to pick up able-bodied idlers and make them give an account of themselves. . . . Olean does not care to harbor a gang of loafers. . . . We'll give them work if they want work. They can get into the army, if they want to fight. They can go to jail, if they won't do either."[2]

◆ ◆ ◆

Camp Upton 12:15pm
Sat. March 2, 1918

Dearest Mother and sister,
      It is one beautiful day, I don't think I will have to drill this afternoon so I'll probably take a walk up the avenue and go sight seeing.
      Well we were sworn into the U.S. service last night and are now considered soldiers although we haven't our uniforms yet, but they think we will get them this afternoon.

Mother I saw one of the most marvelous sights yesterday I ever beheld, it was a review of all the soldiers in Camp Upton, on parade. There were quiet a few notable men here reviewing them, namely Gov. [Charles] Whitman, Pres. Wilson, and staff and officers from the English and French armies. I don't know the exact number of men but I believe there were close to 50,000 men, because we stood for about 3 hrs. watching them go by. This camp is about 2 times as large as Olean, some camp, eh what?

All the boys are getting along with the drills in pretty fair shape, and it makes a fellow feel like a king. We started in on physical culture exercises this morning, which were quiet hard for a few of us old men, but we will soon round up in shape.

This is a great life, mother, if a fellow don't get homesick. I'm not that way yet, but I suppose I will get that way in a few weeks. Mother I enquired about that $15.00 per month that I thought you would get from the government, but they claim down here, that as long as I have a brother home working you cannot get it. So I would advise you to go to the Olean Chapter, Red Cross, and find out for sure. That would be the only way to find out.

They asked all of us what branch of service we wanted to go in, and all the Olean boys took Field Artillery which is the easiest of the whole bunch. Our Lieut. explained the duties of the Engineer, Aviation, Infantry, Field Artillery etc, and we came to the conclusion that F.A. is the best.

Mother we can't kick at all about the way they treat us we get three square meals a day and a good little cot at night what more could a man want.

Now I don't want you to worry about me at all, but take good care of yourself and (the kids) Harry and Helen.

Well I guess I will ring off for now so with love to all.
I remain your loving son,

Frederick
Casual Barracks
Battery F 304th F.A.
Camp Upton

◆ ◆ ◆

Here Fred mentions that he and all the others received their uniforms and other equipment just a few days after arriving at Camp Upton. They were unusually lucky in this regard, for thousands of new soldiers in camps around the country had to wait weeks to get their uniforms. The problem was that the army was expanding faster than factories throughout the country could start producing the clothing, guns, ammunition, telescopes, field telephones, airplanes, and all the other items that would be needed. In some cases new recruits never had rifles or field artillery pieces with which to practice. They received their arms only after arrival in France. Indeed, none of the tanks and few of the cannons used by American troops had been made in America. The AEF relied heavily on equipment made in Britain and France.

Howard's regimental history notes how crucial shortages affected the men. At first, the 304th was scheduled to use 3-inch guns, each pulled by six horses. But there were no 3-inch guns or horses, so the plan was changed to 4.7-inch guns, each to be pulled by a tractor or truck. As it happened, there were few 4.7-inch guns to practice on. Moreover, there were few tractors or trucks either, but dozens of men were put into training on how to drive and repair them. As will be seen further below, plans changed once more upon arrival in France. Howard summarizes the situation this way: ". . . in all the training the imagination played a large part. Everything had to be simulated. It was like little boys playing they were soldiers" (p. 19).

Fred praises the food, both its quality and its quantity. Like many soldiers from humble backgrounds, he ate better in the army than he had ever done before. The army had precisely calculated the dietary needs of the ordinary soldier. In the training camps the average soldier's three daily meals contained a total of 4,761 calories.[3]

◆ ◆ ◆

Camp Upton
3-4-18

Dear Mother,

I think it is about time I should write you a few lines, regarding myself. Mother, all the more I stay around here the better I like it, we have got a bunch of pretty good officers, and they try to do every thing in their power for our comfort, so you need'nt worry about me, which I know you and Helen, and Harry do every day, because I have good companions around me and we do certainly enjoy our selves. Our great hobby is singing, playing cards, checkers, telling stories, or any other thing we can do to amuse ourselves.

We received our uniforms today, and we are some happy gang. Our outfit consists of 1 Regulation Overcoat, 1 Rain coat, 2 full uniforms, consisting of 2 pair's of pants, 2 coats, 3 pair's of underwear, 1 winter cap, which looks like the cap's the Russian Cassacks wear, 1 felt hat for summer use, 2 pairs of shoe's, we haven't got these yet, but will receive them tomorrow, and 1 pair of leggins, also 5 pairs of socks, 2 heavy pair, and 3 medium weight pair. Now thats what I call some outfit, so I suppose I will have to send the rest of my clothes home in a few day's.

We also get some real swell eats, sunday for dinner we had a meal fit for a king. The menu was.

Sliced Peaches
Mashed potatoes with chicken gravey
Fried chicken
Turnips
Cocoa and all the bread and butter you could eat

Now I dont think Uncle Sam, is starving us as some people are saying. It is not only one day, but we have, meat and potatoes, corn, pudding's etc every day, so you see I am not starving.

With the drilling and eats I am getting I will be some man when I come back home.

We had a lovely sunday here, the sun out bright and early, and it stayed out all day. We had two band concerts one at 10:00 in the morning and one at 8:00 in the afternoon, by our regimental band, which is some band, there is about 50 pieces in it.

Tonight we are having a regular Olean winter it is quiet cold and snowing quiet hard. We have been quarantined in the vicinity of our barracks ever since we came here, on account of being new men, for they are on the lookout for disease, etc.

Well mother I will have to close, as the bugle is blowing taps, 9:00 pm, which is the time the lights go out, for we have to go to bed, good by and God bless you all.

> Your Son
> Private Frederick A.
> Kittleman

My address is

> Casual Barracks
> Btry F. 304th F.A.

◆ ◆ ◆

Below Fred refers to a "Lasky" picture. Jesse L. Lasky was one of the pioneering Hollywood movie producers. His 1918 film *Freckles* starred Jack Pickford, brother of Mary Pickford. The movie was shown in the camp's Y.M.C.A. building. That organization proved to be of crucial importance for all the troops, both in America and after their arrival in France. Y.M.C.A. houses and tents provided entertainment, food, cigarettes, newspapers, books, and friendly conversation for the men. Several of Fred's letters were written on Y.M.C.A. stationery. The Knights of Columbus, Jewish Welfare Board, Red Cross, and American Library Association also did their best to supply and comfort the soldiers.

Fred's description in this letter of the inoculation shots that each man received was no exaggeration. Howard's regimental history gives this account:

The needle deserves special mention, for it loomed large in the imagination of the rookie. To the first lot sent it came as a surprise—before the man knew what was happening the needle had been thrust into his arm and the damage was done. But those who came later were greeted all the way from the station with jeering cries of "Wait till you get the needle," "You want to look out for that needle—three men died from it yesterday." For weeks afterward any reference to inoculations in songs or skits at the battery entertainments was sure to bring a laugh. (pp. 11–12)

Despite the fearful inoculations administered to each man, epidemics of measles and other ailments often ran rampant through the training camps. As part of the anti-German sentiment that spread through the country, "German measles" became "Liberty measles."

♦ ♦ ♦

March 8, 1918
Camp Upton N.Y.

Dear Brother,
    Received your most welcome letter this afternoon, but it was a few day's behind, as it was dated March 4. The reason for that, was that you made a mistake, in the Btry. You had btry S and it ought to have been btry F so dont let it occur again.
    The boy's are having quiet a time in the barracks just at present (it is now 5:30 pm). We all received another shot in the arm today, and it certainly was a dandy, as it knocked 4 or 5 of the men

out, and about 2 of the others are shaking like a leaf, I am starting to tremble a little myself. We have got to get another shot in about 8 or 10 days, and it will be worse than this one. I havent explained what these shots in the arm are for yet, have I? Well here goes. They use a hyperdermic needle, shove it in your arm, and let it squirt. It contains serum, or something like that, and is a preventive for measels, scarlet fever, etc. (March 9–18). Every man in camp has got to take the three shots and get vaccinated. My arm is pretty sore this morning, but it will soon wear off.

Oh, the Needle! the Needle! The Pro-phy-lac-tic Needle!

FIGURE 2. The Feared Needle. Reprinted from Howard, *Autobiography of a Regiment.*

Harry you asked me if I say my prayers nights well I do and I havent forgot them once. I could not go to church last sunday on account of our barracks being quarantined in, and I dont think I will be able to go this sunday either. Last night was the first time they let us in the Y.M.C.A. They had a five reel "Lasky" picture, entitled "Freckles" and it was fine, in addition they had Miss Margaret Wilson (pres. Wilsons daughter) who is a swell soprano singer. They also had piano players, violinists, a harpist, and a swell tenor singer all talent from Camp Upton, and they were fine. Believe me they have got some swell musicians in this place.

You asked me about the wrist watch you got me well I have got it regulated and it keep's good time, you also said something about the Olean paper, I only saw one down here and it was a week old, so if you will send it to me, I will appreciate it very much, Well Harry you tell mother that I asked our Leut[enant] about that $15.00 amount that she ought to get and he told me to wait until I got assigned to a regular company and then bring it up to the captain. The Leut. said I ought to get it, so that's a little hope any how.

Well I will close, because I have got to go out and drill in about 10 min.

Give them all my love, well good bye from your loving brother Fred.

P.S. Tell Ma and Helen I will write them a real long letter tomorrow.

◆ ◆ ◆

Below Fred mentions the work that his sister Helen is doing to help the Red Cross. That organization plus other private service groups provided all sorts of services to the troops while in their training camps and later in France: medical care, cigarettes, books, movies, stationery, and such. The Olean newspapers were filled with calls to support these groups. The newspapers also regularly reported on the success of war bond drives. Like people elsewhere in the country, those in Olean were also required to conserve energy sources that might be needed for the war effort. In January 1918 the New York State Fuel Administrator instructed all towns and cities throughout the state to enforce strict regulations to conserve coal, oil, and wood. Although these restrictions were later eased, for a time all businesses and homes in Olean were forbidden to use any outdoor lighting. Olean was to be dark every night except Saturday.[4]

◆ ◆ ◆

Camp Upton N.Y.
March 11, 18

My dear little sister,

So you think my letters are getting very interesting, I think you are the only one that thinks so. I am awfully glad you like your Red Cross work which you started in school. This is the kind of stuff that will help win this WAR, where every body, no matter who he, or she might be, will do there share. As far as you being awkward, you are the only one that thinks so, now get that awkwardness stuff out of your head because you are very clever when you want to be, especially in *lying*. Now dont get mad, I did not mean the *lying* part of it. Helen the first chance I get to get my picture taken in my uniform, I will send you one home and show you I am very clever looking. Oh shish, You said Harry was getting fat, well he ought to, there is one mouth less to feed. You see he is eating his share and mine to. But I tell you he is not the only one getting fat, I am like a young pig.

My arm is getting into pretty good shape and does'nt hurt a bit now. I got my second "Inoculation" friday afternoon, and believe me my arm was pretty sore Friday night and Saturday but its allright now. I will get another ("shot" or) inoculation in about eight or ten days. Well little sweetheart I want Harry to take a good picture of you, then send it to me. I wrote in for a P.R.R. pass from New York to Olean and expect it any day, so as soon as I get a furlough* I will be ready to come home for a while.

From you[r] brother who thinks all the world of you. I wish I could kiss you about 1,000,000 times tripled.

Fred

◆ ◆ ◆

Camp Upton N.Y.
March 19, 1918

Dear Mother,

It seems to be an age since I last wrote home, but its only a couple of days. I received your postal this morning and it was a little reminder, so I am doing my bit tonight. I didn't have time yesterday as I done my weekly wash, and had to work in the kitchen, washing dishes, cleaning off the mess tables, sweep and mop the floors, and help the cook dish out the food. There were four of us detailed on this job. Everyone gets a turn at it so I wont get it again for three or four [days].

---

*Shortly after this Fred apparently did get a pass from his former employer, the Pennsylvania Railroad. On April 18, 1918, the *Olean Evening Herald* listed him as one of 30 Olean men from the 77th Division who arrived home for a brief visit.

We received some very sad news in our quarters this morning, they told a few of the Olean boys that one of our number, "Dot" Moore, died in the hospital from pnewmonia, he had been sick a little over nine or ten days. One good thing his mother will get the $10,000 insurance, which he carried since joining Uncle Sams Army. His mother and his brother John, who works in the Exchange National Bank, came down here last week to see him, but John seeing he was pretty low persuaded his mother to go home, while he remained. I saw John today and he feels pretty bad. I bet they certainly will have some funeral in Olean. No doubt every one in the city will turn out. I wish you would send me the "Olean Times" of that day. Now dont worry about me mother, for I am in the best of health, in fact never felt so good in all my life, I am taking very good care of myself, so dont fret and cause yourself to have a heartache. All the rest of the boys are in good health and pretty happy for there is something going on every minute, so the fellows don't get very lonely.

I think we are going to leave Camp Upton, for some other camp, which is about ten miles from Brooklyn, for a little Artillery practice. There is rumors, that we leave about saturday, though I would not put much faith in these rumors, as we hear an awful lot of them, around this camp.

Say mother I wish you would tell Irene, or rather Mrs Ellis to drop me a line or two, so I could get her address, as I lost the one which she gave me.

What was the matter with her husband, did he get a little jealous or something because I wrote her? Iskabible!* Also, what in the devil ails Anna, that she left Bill and the baby, she must be out of

---

*"Ishkabibble" was a derisive slang term that became popular in the years just before the war. It meant "Who Cares?" or "I should worry?" A cornet-playing comedian who became a famous character in motion pictures and on television in the mid-twentieth century adopted "Ish Kabibble" as his stage name.

her head. Thats the way with most women they dont appreciate a good husband when they get one. I think Bill is far to good for her, and if I was "red", I'd go down to her house and knock the hell out of her brothers for taking the furniture out of the house. Now that he is rid of her, he ought to let her stay with her people, and let them keep her. I'd call it good ridance.

I took out my $10,000 goverment insurance today, and had $15.00 per month alloted to you, and I think the goverment will send $10.00 a month besides, so that will help you out a little. I only wish I could send you more, but the insurance will cost me around $7.00 a month, and I will have the remainder for expense money, not very much to be sure, but enough money for me, as a fellow can't spend very much around here. So I guess I can get along alright.

The weather today was like real old summer day's, and as I didnt have no drilling or work to do, I took a nice long walk in the morning, and played ball in the afternoon.

I received a letter from Helen this morning, and must say she uses a very fine texture of writing paper, better give her a little reprimand, and tell her to use toilet paper the next time she writes. You had better tell Harry not to order the Olean Times for me as several of the fellows receive it every day, and then pass it around to the rest of the fellows so I get it pretty regular. I received a letter from Aunt Mabelle this morning, also a card from Donina Gabler, this was quiet a surprise for me. Well mother, I am running out of ammunition, so I will close hoping to hear from you and the kid's real soon.

Your loving son
Fred.

P.S. Give all the neighbours my best regards. I wish you send me Jen Provins address so I could drop her a line or two.

◆ ◆ ◆

Camp Upton N.Y
Sat. 3-30-18

Dear Mother,

Received your most welcome prize box yesterday, I also rec'd the one Aunt Pauline sent. Now believe me a couple of friends and myself had a great little feast on cookies and candy. I havent cut into the cake yet, as I am saving it for tomorrow.

We had quiet a little fire down here friday morning at about 1:00 am. Every man in camp, had to get up, when the bugle sounded the fire alarm. There was some excitement for a few minutes, but it soon died out. The building in question was a K of C. The loss was approximately $10,000. Luckily, the wind was not blowing, or the whole camp might of went up.

They have been drilling us pretty steady for the last few days. Our drilling consists of pitching shelter tents, packing our haversack's, physical exercises and the manual of arms.

Packing a haversack is quiet a difficult thing for a beginner to do, and do right. We first lay our shelter halves on the ground, next two woolen blankets are folded and placed in the center of the shelter half. On blankets we then place our tent poles, which fold up, and five tent stakes, and a tent rope next comes our bacon can and our condiment can, which contains coffee and sugar. Then comes a pair of under-drawers, and shirt, two pairs of socks, also a rain coat, a towel and our toilet articles. The whole bundle is then rolled up and haver sack straped over it. In top of H.S. [haver sack] is a pocket which contains our mess kits. The whole thing when completed weighs about 60 lbs. It is carried on the back and is held in place by two straps, one [of] which goes over each shoulder. They carry very easily, when adjusted right. Besides this pack a fellow has a cartridge belt and a gun which weighs about 10 lbs.

Well mother this is all for the time, will try to do better in the next letter.

With love to all.
From your loving son
Fred.

♦ ♦ ♦

Camp Upton N.Y.
4-17 1918

Dear Brother,

Received your letter yesterday, and must say you have certainly got an awful line of bull. So you have formed the same opinions of me, as Helen has, in regards to writing letters. Well I'll tell you Harry I do quiet a bit of writing these days, but I am getting a little sick of it.

Our outfit has had it pretty soft all week long. Some of the boys went to New York this morning, I was going at first, but changed my mind. The reason I did not go is that it would cost to much for board and lodging, as they are going to stay over until Tuesday morning. If I thought I could get a drink of beer in little old New York on a Sunday I might of went.

The weather today is simply lovely, so I think I will take a long walk and visit around are ["our"] little, khaki clad, city camp Upton. I might be able to cop off some of the New York girls that come down here on a Sunday. Does Herman Harty still come down with a "snoot full" and talk about his expierance, the good times he had while he sojourned at Camp Dix.

Charlie Moore was here to day from Camp Dix and says all the fellows are feeling fine. He is in the Field Artillery. Guess I will ring off as it is pretty near dinner time. With love to all

Fred.
Pvt. F.A. Kittleman
Btry F 304th F.A.

◆ ◆ ◆

The opening lines of the following letter reveal something important about America's rush to send men to France. Fred was absolutely correct to state that his regiment was insufficiently prepared for warfare. Hence the speculation that they were about to be sent to another camp for additional training. Britain and France, however, were desperately beseeching the United States to send "men, men, men" to Europe as quickly as possible. The horrendous trench warfare that had commenced in 1914 was still dragging on, but the German army had recently initiated a series of offensives that threatened to break through Allied lines. As will be seen in the letter of April 29, the United States acceded to French and British entreaties and sent Fred's poorly trained regiment, along with many others, across the ocean as soon as was possible. The trip to another camp never took place.

◆ ◆ ◆

Camp Upton
4-19-18

Dear Mother,

Just a few lines to let you know I am OK. I think that we are going to move to some Southern training camp within a couple of day's, maybe we will get a furlough to go home, but I doubt it. I think our destination will be Spartansburg S.C. where the New York N.G. are encamped.* It will be anywhere from three to six months before this regiment I am in, will be in fit condition for over sea service, for the simple reason that we have an awful bunch of new men in our battery and it will take some time to train them.

Received money belt yesterday, it is just the thing I need. So I thank you very much.

I received Harry's letter this morning, and had a real good laugh over the way he fed his insect menagerie.** He surely has got an awful lot to learn. If he was at Camp, he would get all this training which is so essential to man.

I would advise you not to write, until I find out for sure, where we are going. I will keep you informed so do not worry, also do not send any packages as I am liable not to get them.

Give my little sister and brother my love and tell them I will write later. Well mother I will close for now, hoping that the letter finds you well and in the best of health.

Your loving son
Fred.

P.S. Do not worry. Am very glad to here you have phone in house, If I get real lonesome will call you up.

◆ ◆ ◆

---

*National Guard

**As will be seen frequently below, having an insect menagerie—body lice—was an even bigger problem for the soldiers.

Below is the first of Fred's censored letters. From this point until his return to America, one of Battery F's officers, the captain or one of the lieutenants, read each of his letters. If the letter revealed nothing specific about the location or activities of Fred's unit, the officer signed the letter or its envelope and let it be sent. In a later letter Fred mentions that many of his letters got sent back to him because they contained too many specifics.

Camp "Sea Breeze" was Fred's humorous way of referring to the ship he was on. It was the USS *Leviathan*. Ironically, Fred was on his way to fight Germans in what had been a German ship. The *Leviathan* had been built in Germany in 1913. Its original name was the SS *Vaterland* (that is, Fatherland), and it was the largest passenger ship in the world. When the war started in 1914, the ship happened to be docked in Hoboken, New Jersey. Fearful of the mighty British navy, the ship's owners kept it immobile in Hoboken for the next three years. The United States seized the ship in April 1917 upon its entry into the war. The renamed vessel then became a troopship, capable of carrying 14,000 men at a time. One U.S. Navy sailor who served on the *Leviathan* later in 1918 was the future Hollywood star Humphrey Bogart. Following the war, the U.S. government sold the vessel to a private company, which refurbished it and made it once again into a luxury transatlantic passenger ship. Carrying the 304th Field Artillery and numerous other regiments, the vessel departed from Hoboken on April 24 and arrived in Brest on May 2.

As Fred says in this letter, he and all the others are eager to get a crack at the Germans. They would have to wait until landing for that, because no German U-boat came near them during the voyage. In fact, not a single American troopship was bothered at all during the war. The Allies had stepped up their convoy system in the spring of 1917, with remarkable success. Ships coming to Europe from the United States, Canada, Australia, or other places generally were escorted by cruisers or other available warships. As soon as the *Leviathan* and other vessels neared European waters they were greeted by American or British destroyers. These latter vessels had two advantages that helped to scare away German submarines: speed and depth charges (large containers holding 300 pounds of dynamite that could be hurled overboard). Numerous Allied land-based airplanes also patrolled European waters on the lookout for enemy submarines. The Allies had stepped up their convoy system in the spring of 1917, and the results were remarkable. A total of 16,539 ships were convoyed across the Atlantic between May 1917 and the end of the war in November 1918. Of that number 16 were lost due to storms or other natural factors, and 36 were stragglers that had fallen too far behind the warships sent to protect them.[5]

◆ ◆ ◆

Camp "Sea Breeze"
Monday, April 29 1918
Somewhere at sea

Dear Mother

Just a few lines to let you know I am feeling OK. No doubt it is quiet a surprise to you to hear that we are on the high seas, sailing for your mother country. It came rather sudden, but all the boy's are very happy over the idea of getting a crack at the Germans. Do not worry at all about me, because I will take the best of care of myself. I am enjoying this ocean trip very much, wish you and the rest of our familie were taking it together.

We probally will have a little trouble in getting our mail, because it will take any where from two to four weeks to reach us, but we should worry eh mother! Just as soon as I reach the other side I will write a real letter to all of [you].

The only trouble we are expierancing is washing ourselves with salt water, believe it is some job to get clean. The ordinary toilet soap's will not even touch the dirt, so we have to use a special soap called salt water soap and with this we only get about half clean. A great game mother, if you don't weaken, and I havent shown any signs of weakening yet, and don't intend to.

Give my love to my dear little sister and brother. Did not receive Helens box of fudge until we were all ready to leave camp Upton. Tell her it certainly was good. Will close with love.

> Your loving Son
> Private Fred. K.
> Btry F 304th F.A.
> A.E.F. via New York

P.S. Give my address to May and tell her I will write later as I am out of stationary. (I had a "helluva" time getting these two sheets)

◆ ◆ ◆

After disembarking from the *Leviathan* in the port of Brest, Fred wrote in his journal that the town's countryside "was the most wonderful scenery that I have ever seen." The 304th Field Artillery immediately marched a few miles outside town to Pontanézen Barracks, which had been a camp used by Napoleon's soldiers. The accommodations there were so primitive that it looked as if no improvements had

FIGURE 3. USS *Leviathan*. This photograph from 1918 shows the ship in the dazzle camouflage paint that it sported during the war. This color pattern made it difficult for enemy ships to spot it. Reprinted from *American Armies and Battlefields in Europe*.

been made since the time of the emperor. There the men rested for five days. On May 7 they boarded trains and spent a day and a half traveling south. In his journal, Fred noted that many men grumbled about their lack of sleep and the cramped conditions in the train. He then added, "Our lieutenant said not to kick, because the worst was yet to come. He was right." Upon detraining, they marched several miles to the camp that would be their home until early July. This camp, which Fred was not allowed to name in his letters, was Camp de Souge, located several miles outside the large city of Bordeaux.

Soon after settling in, the 304th learned that much of their training at Camp Upton was useless. None of the American-made 4.7-inch guns or trucks or tractors that they had been promised would be arriving. Instead, they were given French 75-millimeter field guns, each to be pulled by six horses. So the crews had to learn how to operate an entirely different gun. The 75mm was a light 3-inch field piece, sometimes also called a howitzer, that threw a projectile weighing about 20 pounds up to a distance of 5 miles. It was highly regarded for its accuracy and reliability and its ability to fire more than 15 rounds per minute. The gun became so famous that the "French 75" cocktail was named after it. That cocktail was created in 1915 at the famous New York Bar in Paris (later Harry's New York Bar). Consisting of gin, champagne, lemon juice, and sugar, the drink delivered such a kick that it felt like one was being shelled by the field gun. With horses replacing trucks, the men who had learned to repair motors also now had to learn how to handle and care for animals. But at least they now had real matériel with which to work, for at Camp Upton most of the men had not had an opportunity to fire a gun of any sort.

From May to July of that year, the German army made a series of five offensives along the extensive line of trenches that extended from Belgium to Switzerland. After the Russian Revolution of November 1917 and that country's withdrawal from the war, Germany had been able to withdraw nearly fifty army divisions from the eastern front and throw them at the Allies in the West. Only with staggering losses did British and French troops manage to keep German advances toward Paris to a minimum. Despite this perilous situation for the Allies, only a few divisions of American troops, those with more experienced men from the Regular Army, participated in the fighting. Most of the American divisions were like Fred's 77th, composed of new recruits who needed more training before they could be of much use in the line of fire.

In the letter below, Fred speaks of German prisoners of war and observes that they seem contented and well fed. The whole topic of prisoners of war is a contested one. Both sides in the conflict accused the other of mistreating captured soldiers. By the end of the war there were about 9 million such prisoners in Europe—about 2.5 million in Germany (mostly British, French, and Russian) and 400,000 in France (mostly German). Many of the prisoners were used in forced labor repairing roads or involved in similar work. Others were employed in agriculture. The prisoners whom Fred saw shortly after his arrival in France were in camps far from the fighting and thus were in relatively safe and comfortable lodgings. But both the Allies and the Central Powers were guilty of putting many prisoners to work at the front, where they were housed in unhygienic conditions and sometimes were shelled by the artillery of one side or the other.[6]

Fred is convinced that he is fighting for a righteous cause. By 1918 the majority of Americans, even recent immigrants, had been

Figure 4. The French 75mm Field Gun. Courtesy of Ralph Lovett, Lovett Artillery Collection, lovettatillery.com.

persuaded by government propaganda that this was a fight for democracy and, indeed, for the preservation of civilization itself.

◆ ◆ ◆

May 9, 1918
"Some where in France"

Dearest Mother

Just a few lines to let you know I am alive and still kicking. Havent been able to write, as we have been on the move for the last two weeks. We are now established in a permanent camp, so you will receive letters pretty regular.

We certainly had [a] lovely trip crossing the Atlantic. We expieranced no rough weather at all, the result was, there were only two or three of our outfit that were seasick. I was in great hopes of meeting with some German subs, so our convoys could get a good crack at them, but we did not see a one. Gee it certainly is a grand and glorious feeling, after seeing nothing but water for a couple of weeks, to find yourself firmly established on land again. It sure looked good to all of us.

After landing we were sent to a detention camp for four or five days, and from there put on trains and sent to the camp which we will now make our headquarters for a considerable length of time.

It doesnt seem as if I was over 4000 miles away from home, but never the less it is a fact. Believe me mother, if I ever get out of this, I certainly will have some story to tell.

I have seen an awful lot of German prisoners, and they all seem to be happy and contented. The French do certainly treat them O.K. and they ought to be very grateful, considering the way the Germans treat there prisoners of war.

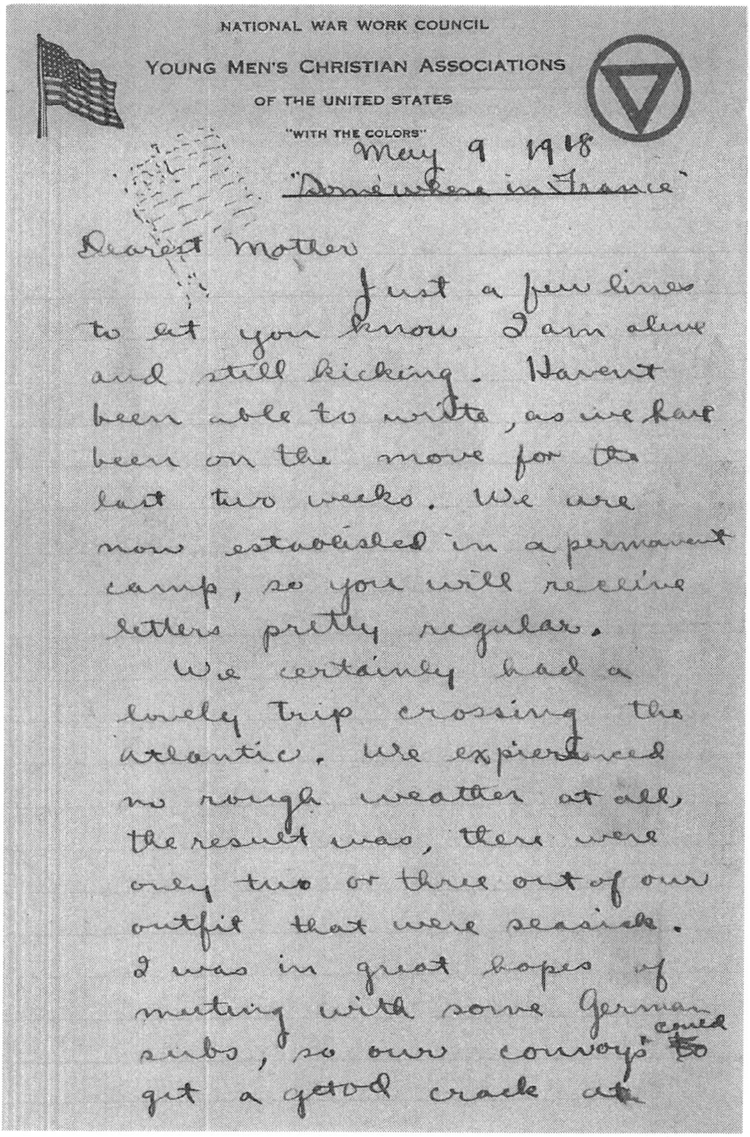

NATIONAL WAR WORK COUNCIL

YOUNG MEN'S CHRISTIAN ASSOCIATIONS

OF THE UNITED STATES

"WITH THE COLORS"

May 9 19 18

"Somewhere in France"

Dearest Mother

Just a few lines
to let you know I am alive
and still kicking. Haven't
been able to write, as we have
been on the move for the
last two weeks. We are
now established in a permanent
camp, so you will receive
letters pretty regular.

We certainly had a
lovely trip crossing the
atlantic. We experienced
no rough weather at all,
the result was, there were
only two or three out of our
outfit that were seasick.
I was in great hopes of
meeting with some German
subs, so our convoys could
get a good crack at

FIGURE 5. First page of letter of May 9, 1918. Courtesy of Kittleman
Collection, St. Bonaventure University Archives.

From what I have seen of the French people, the majority are very poor and their morale condition is very bad. The women have to do pretty near all the work, as the only men that are left around is the men who have been wounded in battle, and sent home to recuperate. All the young men from about fourteen and up are all in the army or navy. So you see that the condition of this country is very bad, so it is a very honourable cause which Uncle Sam is fighting. To free the countries of Europe from autocracy, or bondage as our own President Lincoln freed the slaves from slavery. It is about the same thing.

Well dear mother dont worry or fret about me at all because I am in the best of health, and will see this thing to the finish. Give my love to "sis" and Harry. Will try to write each a line just as soon as I have time. With love to all.

Your loving Son
Pvt Fred A. Kittleman
Btry F 304th F.A.
via N.Y. A.E.F.

P.S. I am enclosing a little Humorous letter which I cut from a paper in the states. I think it is quiet good. Give my best to Mary L. and tell her to write.

◆ ◆ ◆

May 14 1918

Dear brother
Just a line to let you know I am OK. This certainly is a lovely country, that is, as far as I have seen it, but to tell the real truth I

would prefer the good old U.S.A. any time. Here's hoping it isnt very far off either. Will you please send Geo. Fingers* address, so I can communicate with him. With love to all.

Your loving brother

◆ ◆ ◆

We were Learning the Game of War

FIGURE 6. In Training at Camp de Souge. Reprinted from Howard, *Autobiography of a Regiment*.

---

*George Fingers and his family lived just a few houses away from the Kittlemans in Olean. After the war George joined the city's police force and eventually rose to the position of chief.

When Fred wrote "over there" below, he was echoing George M. Cohan's famous song of that name. Cohan composed it shortly after the United States declared war in April 1917. Its most famous phrase was "The Yanks are coming." Cohan's song became wildly popular in both of the world wars.

This is Fred's first mention of his job as a bugler. Battery F had three buglers. They played their horns several times a day, including reveille in the morning, meal times, call to assembly, and taps at night. When in battle at the Front, a bugler's duties became less fixed. Instead of calling men to meals, for example, he needed to alert men when enemy airplanes were sighted overhead. For each purpose a bugler needed to learn a different tune. Fred also was trained to operate the guns. As he states in one of his final letters, during the fighting his job was to help out wherever he was needed.

◆ ◆ ◆

"Over there"
May 16 1918

Dear little sister

Received your letter yesterday, which was sent to Camp Upton, and then transfered to the A.E.F. Your letter was dated April 14 so you see it is over a month old, but nevertheless your letters would be interesting to read if they were a year old, so keep right on writing.

We are in a camp now which seems an awful lot like Camp Upton to me so it seems like home to me. Now for the best part of it. We are given permission to get wine and beer, at the wine gardens which are situated right on the outside of the camp. Our hours for going there is from 6:00 pm to 8:30 pm. The fellows certainly have a good time around these places. The only trouble about this place is when a fellow buy's oranges, chocalate bars etc the French people selling this stuff, take advantage of the American soldiers and sock the devil out of them. For a bar of chocalate, which would cost a dime in the states, we have to pay 25¢, oranges cost us a franc for three about the size of a peach. The value of a franc is about $.18 of our money. This French money, just like the people, is queer stuff to get on to, but I am learning fast.

I suppose mother pretty near had a fit when she received post card stating that I had arrived safely over-sea's. I can just picture her in my mind now, the way she took on, and I believe you were almost as bad. How about it "sis". Well kid, dont worry a bit, because your brother is in the best of health and likes his bugle job immensley. I have got to practice from 8:00 am to 11:30 am and from 1:00 pm until 5:00 pm, but it is a lot better than drilling. This is some place camp "sis", and it is only about 15 miles from a pretty good sized city. Sorry I cannot mention the name, but when I get back home again you will get a full account of all my travels abroad. Hoping to hear from you soon.

> Your loving brother
> Pvt Fred K.
> Btry F 304th F.A.
> A.E.F. via N.Y.

P.S. Give my love to Aunt Pauline, and "Red". Ant Fanny and dont forget Mother and Harry.

◆ ◆ ◆

304th Field Artillery
May 20 1918

Dear Mother,

Just came in from a taking a nice little swim, in what they call a lake around this part of the country, in reality it is nothing more than a pond, but the water is just fine, so it makes a fellow feel pretty good after being in the hot sun all day.

The weather has been very hot for the last week. It gives a fellow the spring fever, making him feel very lazy, but whether we are lazy or not we have to keep right on with our work. Cheer up kid! The war will be over sometime, by the way things are going now it will be over sooner than any of us expected. Hears hoping.

This is [a] good camp in which we are now situated. It reminds me an awful lot like Camp Upton. The only trouble it makes it a little difficult drilling, as the ground is very sandy, every time a fellow takes a step he sinks up to his ankle in the sand. Outside of that, this place suits me to a T. Another lovely feature of this camp is the wine gardens which they have established for the American troops. Here *light* beers and wine are obtainable every evening from 6:00 until 8:30. Although I do no cater to this stuff very much as I am a staunch W.C.T.U. never the less I drink all that comes my way.*

I received eight letters and a couple of cards Friday evening, but they were all a month old, so did not contain very much news from the old burg. This writing business is the most hateful thing in

---

*Fred obviously is joking when he says he belongs to the Women's Christian Temperance Union.

Army life to me, as I don't know what to say, but I will give you a better one next time. Give Harry and "sis" my love.

Your loving son
Pvt F.A. Kittleman
Btry F. 304th F.A.
A.E.F. via N.Y.

◆ ◆ ◆

Below Fred reports that many "Chinamen" are working in his camp. These laborers were part of the 140,000 Chinese, mostly peasants, who voluntarily came to France during the war. Because so many British and French able-bodied men were busy fighting, the Allies needed workers for a variety of essential jobs: digging trenches, assembling artillery shells, transporting munitions, repairing roads, delivering food and water, and working in factories. Many of these workers saved their pay and returned to China after the war, but a large number remained in Europe and established immigrant communities in Paris and other cities. Fred looks down on these Asian workers and thus shares the prejudice common among most Americans and Europeans of that era. One of the other soldiers in the 304th wrote home that "These Chinks can get more rest out of a shovel than I can get out of a feather bed."[7] Recent studies of the thousands of Chinese workers in France indicate, however, that, despite the cultural and linguistic barriers, the great majority of them made valuable contributions to the war effort.[8]

◆ ◆ ◆

"Sunny France"
5-25-18

Dear Mother

As it is Saturday afternoon, and I have no bugle practice, I will devote part of the time to write a letter home.

I have been practicing pretty hard for the past week, and a few more weeks like it, I ought to be able to make a bugle talk. I think this job is quiet a lot better than drilling on the guns, also easier. All buglers in light Field Artillery carry side arms (revolver) and get a horse to ride upon. We havent the horses at this writing, but expect them most any day.

This is a very interesting camp, to see, as there are quiet a lot of German, Austrian, and Turkish prisoners. The French keep them pretty busy keeping the roads in repair, or any other work which is so essential to military life. They are treated in a different manner than the prisoners which the Germans take. The French government gives them 2 Franc's a day, good food, and a bed to sleep on at night, and they are all happy that they are prisoners. We also have quiet a bunch of chinamen who do the same work, but they get higher wages, about 7 Franc's a day, which is pretty good money in France. They are the worst class of people I have ever seen. The rest of the camp is composed of American troops, and a finer bunch of men could never be seen. There is also a few French troops, those who have been wounded in battle. This camp is situated about two day's ride behind [the] firing line, so we are as safe here, as if we were in the states so do not worry at all. All the boy's, including myself, are happy and contented, and make the best of it, although it gets a little discouraging at times, we try to do our best for Uncle Sam. The way I have this war doped out is, that a couple of months more will put the finishing touches on the "dutch." Let's hope that my dope is correct. Now a little question mother have you ever heard word from the old gent?* Well I guess I have tired you out reading, so will bring this bunch of unadulterated meadow dressing to a close. Give Helen and Harry a few kisses and tell them to look happy. Would like to write each one, but my vocabulary is very limited. Give all the neighbours. my best regards and don't forget aunt Pauline, and grandpa Edel.** Gee but I'll bet he would give anything if he could only be in the French army, so he could get a crack at the dutch. You know how much love he has for them. Give Mrs. "Irene" Ellis my best and tell her I will send the most lovable letter I can compose. Do this on the Q.T. when Mr isnt around.*** Well mother, will close with love to all.

> Your loving son
> Fred A. Kittleman
> Btry F. 304th F.A.
> A.E.F.

◆ ◆ ◆

---

*Fred's father.

**Xavier Edel was Josephine's father. He and his wife Eugenia, along with their nine children, moved from Alsace-Lorraine to Olean in 1890. Josephine, born in 1874, was one of the older children in the family. Alsace-Lorraine was a region in eastern France that had been seized by Germany in the Franco-Prussian war of 1870–71. The Edels held a grudge against Germany, and that might be the main reason why they eventually moved to America. France regained the region at the end of World War I.

***"Do this on the Q.T." means "Do it secretly." As can be seen from Fred's letters, he was friendly with numerous Olean girls, including at least one married lady whose husband might become jealous. At the front of his journal, Fred listed eight young women along with their addresses in Olean. The woman he eventually married, however, was someone he met upon his return from France.

France

June 6, 1918

Dear Mother,

Will write you a few lines to let you know that I am in the very best of health, and sincerely hope that this letter will find you the same. This also includes Harry and Helen. I dont know what is the matter with you people at home, as I havent heard from you in over a month and a half. The last letter I received was dated April 20-18. So I think you had better get busy. If there is any trouble such as sickness etc please let me know, as I can at least send my sympathy.

The weather is quiet hot and it seems to be getting warmer every day. Rain around this place is almost a miracle. Since I have been on this side it has only rained once, and then only for about five minutes. But everything in consideration this isnt such a bad place after all. We get 30 bucks a month plus 10% for oversea service which brings it up to $33.00. A bed to flap on at night, and some pretty good eats. To tell the truth I am getting as fat as a pig, a soldiers life isnt as bad as some people make it, as there is always two sides to the story. Mother, has A. Harvey, F. Whittenberg, or F. Wiedman been drafted yet? If they havent tell them to write a line or so.

I am getting along real good on my bugle, in fact I have to study hard or I would get put out of the bugle school. Another reason for my trying hard is, that a bugler has it quite a lot easier than the majority of the fellows. My motto in the army is where there's a will, there's a way, and I try to live up to this.*

---

*Fred exaggerates the "ease" of being a bugler. A bugler played an important role both before and during a battle and was held to high standards. Moreover, Fred had to do his part with the gun battery when called upon. Finally, as he soon discovered, he would experience all the physical discomforts and dangers of the other soldiers.

Mother have you received the allotment money from the government, if you havent I will find out what the trouble is, and let you know. Well I think I will have to ring off for now as I cannot think of much more to say. Will try and do better next time.

> Your loving Son
> Fred
> Pvt. F.A. Kittleman
> Btry F 304th F.A.
> A.E.F.

P.S. I will send a card to grandpa Edel, written in French. I think he will be highly pleased in getting it.

◆ ◆ ◆

> France
> June 25 1918

Dear Sis,

Well "butch" received your letter today and was certainly glad to get it, as your letters certainly put the pep in a fellow. Never mind these [piano] exercises you are always telling about, get busy. We will let this matter drop for all times. So dont let it happen again.

Harry was telling me he was going to have you finish your music career with Prof. Wright. Now you want to study very hard. Do not waste any time at all, and when I get home I will have you give me a sample of your work and remember, it wants to be above par, or you will get the worst balling out you ever got. Do not laugh because I mean every word I say. Enough said.

Talk about a musical Johnny. I believe you are trying to kid me "sis". All right I will get one on you next time.

Say kid! Call my little Mary up on the phone, and tell her you just received a letter from your b[r]other, and he said all kinds of lovable things about her. Kid her along, understand and then tell me in the next letter what she said. Give her a good line of Bull. Her phone number is 418J.

Another thing give Irene Ellis my love and ask her if she received my letter which I wrote about one week ago.

Now about your school work. Do a little studying so you will pass your regents this month. Do not write and tell me that you failed, because if you do I will certainly raise an awful rumpus. You know me eh?

You wrote about seeing motion pictures of the 304th F.A. Was it the picture, where the colors and regimental flag's were blessed? If so you might have seen me, with the rest of the buglers parading behind our regimental band. It certainly was an inspiring sight. Well sister Taps is now being blown, so will have to end quickly and hit the hay.

Will close with all the love the censor will allow me to send,

Your loving brother
Fred

P.S. Am enclosing you a little souvenir postal.

Bugler F.A. Kittleman
Btry F 304th F.A.
Amex Forces via N.Y.

◆ ◆ ◆

France
July 1 1918

Dear Mother,

Will drop you a few more lines to let you know I am still sticking around. I am in the best of health and feeling fine.

The weather here is very warm, and as a result I have taken on an awful coat of tan, being almost as dark as a negro.

We wore our campaign hats up to a week ago. They were then taken away, and a summer cap issued. The summer caps are very near the same style, as the cap which I wore when I went home on furlough, but are made of very much lighter material.

Had my picture taken a week ago, one which I will enclose. The other fellow is Louie Nobles from East Olean. And the nurse is a little French maiden, whom we elected to put on [a] Red cross uniform. Rather a nice looking girl, do you not think so? We certainly have a great time around this place, something going on every minute.

I also sent [a] pillow top today, so if nothing happens you will receive it about the same time as this letter. Believe me mother it certainly is a "beaut". I think that a few of the neighbours will envy you in having such a lovely piece of workmanship.

Gee! mother the old burg must be pretty dead with all the young fellows gone, but I dont think it will be for long, because I think a couple of months more, and the Huns will get the worst beaten, any country ever got. So do not worry at all. We will all hope for the best.

> Will close with love and
> kisses for all.
> Your loving Son
> Fred

P.S. Give Moe, Mr & Mrs Cain, Sarah English, Lears and the rest of the folks my best regards and if I have time will write to each of them.

Bugler F.A. Kittleman
Btry F 304th F.A.
Amex Forces
via N.Y.

◆ ◆ ◆

FIGURE 7. Louie Nobles, the "little French maiden," and Fred. Courtesy of Robert Deckman.

Some where in Gods
country
July 7 1918

Dear little bunch of orange blossoms,

Will take a few minutes of my valuable time to drop you that much neglected letter which I promised you.

Well "sis" how is the world using you these days, OK. I hope so anyhow. I suppose you are in the heighth of your ambition now, since school has closed for the summer months.

But there is one thing you must not neglect and that is your music, so practice about four or five hours a day and it will help you considerable.

Say kid that was a great stunt you pulled off at Havens. Believe me I had a pretty good laugh over that, but dont do it again, or I am liable to ball you out.

Well sis will close this letter with all the love and kisses I can give you.

Your effectionate brother
Fred

P.S. Will write a real letter in a week or so.
xxxxxxxxxxxxxxxx [kisses]
Wish they were real.

◆ ◆ ◆

Fred does not mention in this letter that the entire 304th Field Artillery, including its French 75s, had marched to Bordeaux and made a triumphant parade through town on July 4, greeted by enthusiastic crowds. Just two days after writing this letter, Fred and his regiment would depart from Camp de Souge for their first taste of battle. Fred notes the aches he suffers from his training in horseback riding. He is mistaken when he says he will constantly be horseback from this point on. When at the Front, he would have made an easy target for the Germans if he had been riding around out in the open. Moreover, on at least some occasions, when the regiment marched from one location to another he was on foot like most of the others, carrying a heavy sack on his back.

◆ ◆ ◆

France
7-7-18

Dear Mother,

Will drop you a few lines to let you know that I received the "Olean Times", which you sent me, they sure did look good to me, so if it is not to inconvenient for you, kindly send a few more. Although the news was pretty stale, some of it interested me very much. You know mother it makes a fellow [feel] pretty good when he can see what is going on in the "burg". Especially it tells about all the old maids getting married.

Well mother I am OK and in the best of health at this writing and hope that this will find you the same.

I am a little sore, from riding a horse, but this will soon wear off. After we get to the battle front I will be in the saddle constantly, so I am trying my best to be a good horseman.

The boy's are anxiously waiting for the time, when we will be able to get a crack at the Huns, and believe me when battery F. 304th ever gets started there certainly is going to be something doing. Leave it to the old "Keystone" battery.*

I think we have one of the finest bunch of men in the whole regiment, every one a jolly good fellow, and willing to give, or do anything for any man in the whole outfit. This kind of team work, on the part of American soldiers in France, will win this big world's war.

I saw in the "Times" about Co. I [of] N.Y.N.G., (or otherwise 108 inf) landing in France.** Gee but I certainly would like to see them, as I have some very dear friends in this outfit. I think I know where they are located, but of course cannot put it down in writing. No doubt I will run across a few of them in the near future. Here's hoping any how.

Well mother will have to close for now, with love and best wishes for all.

> Your loving Son
> Fred
> Bugler F.A. Kittleman
> Btry F. 304th F.A.
> Amex Forces via N.Y.

◆ ◆ ◆

---

*It is not known why Fred refers to his unit as the Keystone battery. Battery F was composed mostly of men from New York State. Pennsylvania was the Keystone State, and its National Guard division (the 28th) came to be called the Keystone.

**New York National Guard.

[undated]

Dear brother

Just a few lines to let you know I am still living and very much full of life. In the last three or four letters which you have sent me you asked me more questions about different things. You are getting worse than the guy who takes up the state census, but seeing that you are a very near kin of mine I will endeavor to answer a couple anyhow. Bertha H. has not written and I am dam glad, as that is one less to contend with. Any fellow that goes in the army, ought to bring a private secretary along with him to answer his correspondence. Because its some tedious job, writing the same thing every day. The next about the rupture. It is OK and doesnt bother me at all. The doctors treat it very lightly, so I don't think it amounts to very much. If it was very bad I would have been operated on long ago. So you and mother ease up your mind a little on that.*

You also told me to write to Rose Miller, which I did, and if she dont want to answer, she can go to H – H – H – H – H – H (stammer to get effect) Halifax, god I had an awful time trying to get that out. Another thing I wish to bawl you out about is that, you are always complaining about me writing interesting letters to my friends, and when I write home there is nothing in them as they are to dry. I don't see how you make that out, but in my next letter to you I will try and give you a real line of Bull. So look out you don't step in it and go up to your neck. From your loving brother.

Fred

◆ ◆ ◆

*The nature of this rupture is unknown. If he mentioned this in a previous letter, that letter is now missing.

FIGURE 8. Fred "Over There." Courtesy of Robert Deckman.

On July 12 the 304th Field Artillery and most of the 77th Division arrived at the Baccarat sector of the Front in the western foothills of the Vosges Mountains in Lorraine—about 240 miles east of Paris. The 77th Division was the first of the National Army divisions to see action. On July 14 the artillery batteries fired their first shots at the enemy. Though American and German cannons fired some shells at each other virtually every day, this sector had been relatively quiet since 1914. Both the Allies and the Germans tended to send newly-trained units to this area, where they could get a taste of battle before being sent to sectors where the fighting was more fierce. The 77th remained here until August 1. As will be seen here, Fred omits to mention to his mother that he is now in a battle zone.

On several occasions in his letters Fred assures his family that he is safe and states that the doughboys (that is, the infantrymen in the front lines) are the troops in the most danger. Although it is true that fatality rates for the infantry were higher than those of other soldiers, the troops in artillery units were far from safe. Indeed, oftentimes the German artillery units aimed their guns specifically at the Allied and American artillery. Fred's battery, like all others, was usually situated at least a couple of miles behind the front line. But just as the French 75s guns that the Americans had could hurl their shells several miles behind German lines, so also German heavy guns could reach American artillery placements. Hence, upon reaching a new location, the 304th had to find a spot where it would be shielded as much as possible from enemy fire.

An artillery unit was a complex organization. In addition to the 200 men, Battery F included more than 100 horses. The horses pulled the guns plus the wagons that carried food, spare parts, ammunition, and a multitude of other supplies. Dozens of men were especially charged with operating, transporting, and repairing the French 75 field guns, while perhaps an equal number cared for the horses, which needed to be fed and shod, and whose tack needed constant cleaning and repair. There were also cooks, buglers, signalers, topographers, and telephone operators. The field telephones generally were used for communication with men stationed a couple of miles in front of the artillery. These men were charged with locating the enemy's troops or artillery and then relaying that information back to the gun batteries. Wires had to be laid on the ground between the telephones. Those wires frequently were trampled on by human or equine feet or by wagon wheels, thus necessitating time-consuming repairs.

The officers and noncommissioned officers needed skill in mathematics, especially geometry. Determining the angle at which a gun should fire required complex formulas involving the distance from the target, the kinds of shells being fired, and current weather conditions. All of this became even more difficult when the troops were constantly on the move, as they would be in the final months of the war.[9]

◆ ◆ ◆

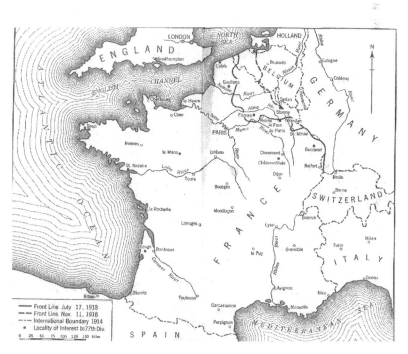

FIGURE 9. Reprinted from *77th Division: Summary of Operations in the World War*.

July 23 1918
France

Dear Mother,

Received you letter yesterday, which was dated June 23, together with money order. This is something, as I told you before, I want you to stop, as I am now in a place where we have very little time in which to spend our money. I assure you that I appreciate it very much, but I have got so many "franc's "in my pocket now, that I can hardly move. So please discontinue practice. If I need any money I will not be a bit bashful about asking for it. You know that from past expierience.

I met another friend of mine yesterday, Nino Pattituce, he is about twenty minutes walk from the place I am in. Army life certainly agrees with him, because he is looking better than I ever saw him look. He stopped at our place and had a little feed. It makes a guy feel pretty good when he see's all his old friends.

Another little thing I want to tell you about, which no doubt will be a little amusing to you.

As I told you in the last letter, we are camping out in our dog tents, and sleeping on the ground.* Well, the other night, I woke up quiet suddenly the cause of all the trouble was that my pet menagerie broke loose, and were crawling all over me, their were four or five mice, and about a dozen June bugs believe me their was some scattering for a few minutes, as shoes, mess kit and everything other thing that was in reach of me was flying at these pests.** Its a great life if you don't weaken.

---

*That letter is missing.

**"Pet menagerie" refers to lice in particular. These were a constant nuisance for Fred and the hundreds of thousands of other soldiers. The problem became even worse once they arrived at the Front, where it was impossible to take a hot bath or wash one's clothes.

Well mother I received a letter from the old gent, he seemed very tickled in receiving [my] address from you. As it is getting pretty dark, will have to discontinue writing.

From your loving Son
Fred

P.S. Give Harry & Helen my best. Will write a little later. Love to all the neighbours.

Bugler F.A. Kittleman
Btry F 304th F.A.
Amex Forces via N.Y.

◆ ◆ ◆

The gap between Fred's previous letter and this one reflects the fact that the 77th Division was now an active participant in the war. Soldiers had much less time to correspond with friends and family. On August 1 the 77th departed from Baccarat and spent the next twelve days traveling northwest by foot and by train to the more active Vesle sector. This brought them near the city of Fismes, 85 miles northeast of Paris. The men had some rest stops along the way. In his journal Fred writes that on August 9 he was paid a total of 65 francs. He went to a nearby village to celebrate with sherry, brandy, cognac, and champagne: "Oh but I had a lovely bean on me next morning. I am now under arrest, because I left camp the night before without permission. Believe me it was worth it anyway. I don't know what they are going to do with me, but I am not worrying as there is about 20 men besides myself." One can surmise that their officers gave them a tongue lashing, but there is no evidence that Fred and the others received any sort of punishment. When he was discharged from the army, his records indicated that he had never been A.W.O.L or absent from his duties. For obvious reasons, Fred did not write about this episode in his letters to home.

As the 77th neared the Vesle sector, Fred put this in his journal on August 12: "We passed many graves of soldiers both American, Germans and French. The roads all along the route were hardly passable on account of shell holes. The villages all along were wrecks from shell fire. In some places the smell from the bodys of dead horses and men was almost unbearable. Their certainly must of been a regular hell on earth when the marines drove the Germans through this territory." Censors would not have allowed him to put such graphic reports in his letters. Nor would Fred have wanted to disturb his family with bloody details like these.

In this letter Fred is curious about the rising wages of machinists at the railroad and jokes that he would be rich if still back home in his old job. In a later letter (February 25, 1919) he also asks about women taking over factory jobs while men like himself are in France. Although Fred seems to take these sorts of things with good humor, thousands of other veterans would return to America bitter about how their service to Uncle Sam had been a burden to them financially. These feelings would lie at the root of the Adjusted Compensation campaign of the 1920s. More on this in the Epilogue.

◆ ◆ ◆

August 19, 1918
At the Front, France

Dear Brother,
Received your most welcome, letter today. (Letter No: 10) The letter which you said you wrote July 4 (or by the number) letter No:

9 has not reached me to date. No doubt it is still on its way. Let us hope so anyway.

The weather over here is getting somewhat chilly especially the early hours of the morning. I think the weather here is a little bit earlier than what it is in the states. Believe me boy I'd hate to put a winter in this country, if we had to stay on the firing line.

So mother and Helen have gone to visit Aunt Freida, well I think this trip will do both of them a world of good. Wish I were their to show them around New York, Coney Island and a few more of these famous summer resorts. I believe I would enjoy it equally as much as either one of them. Do you not think so?

I received a letter from Helen this morning, and she wrote me quiet an interesting episode about her trip especially her little sailor friend. Well bud, she says you have been kidding her along because she can not get a fellow, but she is going to show you a thing or two from now on. You know bud, "forewarned is forearmed" so kindly take this little tip from me.

The reason you havent heard from me in so long is because I did not have very much time in which to write, another reason is the closer to the front a fellow gets the more difficult it is to send or receive mail. But Uncle Sam is trying his best to overcome these difficulties. So watch out from now on because you are liable to be flooded with mail from me. Ahem! I guess not.

No brother I have not had my head shaved yet because I do not carry a private zoo, but you cannot tell when God will have it so.* If I do get them I suppose that is about the best way to get rid of them. I have written G. Finger, but haven't received an answer

---

*Since writing the previous letter Fred must have had a chance to visit a delousing station, where he would have taken a hot bath and had his clothes cleaned.

so far, as for Louis Hartweg, I wish you would send me his address, because I would like to get in communication with him. I understand he is also "some where in France."

Another thing I wish you would do is send me every list of draftee's that leave Olean. You know I have a bunch of friends around that place, so I would like to keep a little posted on what is going on. So kindly favor this small request of mine.

So Ester Sirdevan told you about writing to her brother Pat. Well this is true enough but I think you are getting a little too personal, when you go monkeying around my friends sister. I thought I had her copped off, and now you come along, and try to beat my time. Better cut it out boy, or you and I will have a battle royal. You tell Pat that I will feel real sorry if he has to go because it is not an easy game. Like our noble Mayor (Foster Studhoemey) would say "Let well enough alone."* This is no joke. No I have not received Pats letter yet. You know Harry that Pat is one of the best friends I have got. I only wish he were hear in France with me, because we certainly could slap up the "vin rouge" (red wine) and vin blanc (white wine). The only trouble at present is that we cannot get any at all, so I am growing a little stale, but "where there is a will there is a way." So I guess I will have to start on a little scouting trip and find some.

You wrote about that doings you had Monday night August 8th, well kid it was a fine layout all right, but if you had a little of the wines I have just mentioned, I think it would of been far more enjoyable. You said you and Leo were <u>alone</u> with the alone underscored. Well who in h.... were the girls, are you afraid to tell their names. You are getting pretty secretive all of a sudden, can't you trust me any more. Slip it to me easy kid, I am still listening.

---

*Foster Studholme, Mayor of Olean, 1916–1919.

No wonder Bertha H. gets sore at you, when you go pulling stunts like that. I suppose I had better cut balling you out, because you are liable to get mad and tear this letter up before you read it all, and my labor will be worth nothing at all.

You sure picked out a real good place to take your meals. Is Mark Hannon still boarding there? Give him my best, also Mr. Hartz.*

Received your blanks which you had enclosed in letter, and lost no time at all in having them filled out. One of my officers 1st Lieut. Pfaelzer witnessed my signature. That sure is some back pay for one month. Just imagine it $67.35. How much do I get for the first 22 days of February? I am getting pretty wealthy since I joined the army. Eh What? gee bud, the machinists must be making, a pretty good stake since they received the government increase. Will you kindly inform me, as to the average pay they are now drawing? I can plainly see I am losing a young fortune since I have been in the army. If I were home now, I could be sporting around town like a young "John D" [Rockefeller]. Dont worry about me being timid about writing for money, You ought to know me of old. The trouble is I cannot even spend the money I am earning in the army, so why write for more.

qt. [Question] You asked me if I go to Mass? ans. Yes every time I get a chance. I always say my prayers, but I find <u>swearing</u> a difficult matter to cultivate in the army.**

---

*Harry still lived at home with his mother and sister, and that is where Fred mailed letters to him. However, he took some meals at a nearby boarding house, perhaps because it was near the rail yard where he worked.

**The regimental chaplain was James M. Howard, who wrote the official regimental history soon after returning to the United States. Howard's book notes that on occasion there were church services for Catholics and Jews. Neither Howard, nor Fred Kittleman, nor anyone else reported any religious frictions between men of different religions.

Well brother as I cannot think of any more to write at present, will close this brief note with love to all.

Fred.
Bugler F.A. Kittleman
Btry F. 304th F.A.
Amex Forces via N.Y.

P.S. Give all the neighbours, Sarah English, Irene Ellis, Mrs Lear, Mrs Finger and May L and any more you can think of my best regards.

P.S. Dont forget Aunt Pauline and Grandma and Grandpa. Its getting quite dark so will prepare for bed.

Good night
Happy dreams bud.

◆ ◆ ◆

The 77th Division fought in four sectors from June to November 1918. The first was Baccarat (June 21 to August 4), the second was along the Vesle River near Fismes (August 12–17). When Fred wrote the following letter, the 77th was engaged in the third sector, on the Oise and Aisne rivers, likewise close to Fismes (August 18 to September 16). The fourth sector, the Meuse-Argonne campaign, will be discussed further below. The fighting became more intense as the division moved from one area to another. Fred's journal gives brief accounts of what the fighting was like for Battery F.

On August 21 he helped to bury a man from his battery, "amongst [a] shower of German shells some coming very near us 7 other graves being nearby."

On August 24 one of his sergeants "was killed while trying to get under cover from German planes. He crawled under an allied plane which had been brought down a few days before. A German shell struck near [the] plane exploding gasoline tank. Sgt. W. and a couple of men from another battery were burned to death, besides six being injured."

On August 25: "Three more of our boys were killed, together with three wounded. This makes a total of 5 men killed and 8 wounded. This position was being shelled by the Hun at a furious speed. All of them coming uncomfortably close. They also sent over mustard sneeze and tear gas. The boys who were killed were buried on the spot (where they met their misfortune) in a downpour of rain."

On August 26: "We are now giving the Germans an intense artillery fire day and night."

◆ ◆ ◆

Aug. 27, 1918
At the Front, France

Dear Brother,

I have received all your mail up to date. Letter #12 being the last. I have had two of these blanks all ready signed, but will enclose two more in case you do not receive the others. You know the way the mailing facilities are at present, its very uncertain, so I guess its best to play "safety first".

Received a letter from Ambrose H[arvey] the other day. He thinks he will be over on this side in a couple of weeks. From what I got out of his letter, I think he is driving an ambulance.

So grandpa received card which I had written in French? Well if he was so well pleased as you say, I'll try to write a little letter, that is, if I can get some one to translate it for me. To tell you the truth this French does'nt interest me a bit, and another we haven't much opportunity to study it. It certainly is amusing to see some of the fellows trying to buy provisions etc from some of the French shopkeepers. They use their hands, much in the same manner a Jew would when he is trying to sell something. For instance, when they go after eggs they'll yell egg's, of course the Frenchy will not understand, then the boys start crowing, cackling like a hen etc. until some kind brother-in-arms comes along, and [helps]them out by saying, "Madame, Donnez-moi six des oeufs, sil vous plait," which means. Madam will you please give me six eggs. It sure is tough on the guys at times, especially when he see's something real good and doesn't know how to ask for it.

So you and Clara are OK again. Well bud if I were you, and had it as bad as you've got it I think I would do the next best thing and get married. Do you not think this is a good idea?

Gee kid you certainly must be up to snuff, when you wear all the good duds [that is, clothes] I left behind, and then buy some more to "boot". No wonder the girls fall for you. Oh Slush! I think I have water on the brain.*

The Pennsy** at Olean must be awful hard up for machinists when they take them, like they have in the last gang of draftees. Have they got many girls working the machines? Is my old girl still on the job? Id like to be back their for a while to see how things are running. So big "narrow guts" W.J. Taylor, our old G.F. has received a better job at Balwins [Baldwin] Loco. works? Well I dont think the men will shed many tears over his departure. I think this is a blessing for some of the men. Who is the new Gen'l Foreman? Kindly let

---

*Harry had numerous girlfriends but never married.

**The Pennsylvania Railroad.

me know as I am interested. Another thing before I forget it. Look over my machinist tools, and see they do not get rusty. Rub a little vaseline on them, because they are a little to valuble to let them get ruined by rusting. I think mother knows where I put my tool box. Do not forget this.

I wish you would tell me who the different people are that ask about me so frequently. Are they chicken, or old married women?

No I have not heard from Louie H[artweg], but without a doubt he is on the firing line, because they need all the men they can get. What branch of the service is he in, the infantry, or artillery? Believe me the dough boys have a pretty rough job of it these day's. This bugler job I have got used to be pretty soft, but at the front every body does his share, to lick the Hun, and take it from me we certainly have got them going. I would like to tell you where we are at, etc but they are so strict in censoring the letters that it is a very difficult proposition to write. I have wrote several letters at different times, but had them all given back; for little things I had in them. This causes a lot of inconvenience, as we have to rewrite the letters omitting part which censor cuts out.

Well brother my mind is wandering so will bring this letter to an abrupt close.

Your loving brother
Fred.

P.S. give my love to Mother and Sister. Will write in a couple of days. Give the neighbours my best wishes.

Bugler F.A. Kittleman
Btry F 304th F.A.
Amex Forces via N.Y.

After several weeks of intense combat in the Oise-Aisne sector, the 77th was relieved on September 14 by an Italian division. The 77th then spent the next ten days marching toward the Argonne forest, some 70 miles to the southeast, and stopping for a few days of rest along the way. As Fred notes in this letter, he is billeted in a farmer's barn.

The gap of several weeks between the previous letter and this one happened at least in part because Fred was too busy fighting to have time for letters. His terse journal entries reveal his feverish activity. Some examples:

Sept 6

2:00 am started in hot pursuit of Germans but our progress was very slow on account of the congested condition of the roads. Troops moving all in the same direction. The roads are filled with shell holes making it very difficult to move ahead. 6:00 am Our outfit crossed the Vesle river on an improvised bridge which was being built by the engineers. The German stronghold was at the top of the hill. All along from the Vesle river to the top of the hill were the bodys of Americans and Germans, which on account of the speed the Germans were retreating had not been buried. I wonder how long it will be before I am the same way. It was a night which I never will forget the longest day I live.

Sept 10

We are firing an intense artillery fire, which the Germans are also doing, some of their shells dropping uncomfortably close to our positions.

Sept 11

Last night "Gerry" came over with an aerial squadron, and made things pretty warm for us for a little while. I don't mind dodging shells but bomb is a different thing.

Sept 14

We are firing a terrible barrage on the Germans. We fired 783 shells per gun. Barrage lasting 8 hrs. . . . I saw a very nice aero battle this p.m. 3 Hun and Allied. They were about 150 feet above us. We were in extreme danger from machine gun fire, but stayed out to watch who came off victor.

The passage of weeks between his letters might also have had another cause. After Fred returned home to Olean, he eventually told his mother, brother, and sister that he had been gassed twice. On numerous occasions he had to rush to put on his gas mask to avoid being injured, but on two occasions the gas got to him before he had any warning. We know the date of the second incident, as will be seen further below. He makes no mention of being gassed anywhere in his journal or his letters, but the first incident might have occurred in late August or early September. Whenever it happened, Fred was one of the lucky ones. He apparently did not go to a hospital, where many men died or were laid up for weeks with the aftereffects.

At The Hague Conference of 1899 most of the major world powers, including Germany, had pledged never to use chemical weapons in warfare. The United States, however, refused to sign the accord. The American delegate, Captain A. T. Mahan, criticized the agreement as hypocritical. He declared, "It is illogical to be tender about asphyziating [sic] men with gas when all are prepared admit that it is allowable to blow the bottom out of an ironclad at midnight, throwing four or five hundred into the sea to be choked by the water."[10] His words proved prophetic, given that both sides were to make extensive use of deadly chemicals in the war that erupted in 1914.

The poison gas that the Germans used came in three varieties, each denoted by the color of the cross or star painted on the outside of the canister. Green gas was an asphyxiate containing phosgene; one deep inhalation of this could lead to death. Blue gas contained an arsenic compound; it caused sneezing, headaches, and nausea, but rarely death. Yellow gas came to be called mustard because of its mustard-like smell; it could cause severe damage to eyes and lungs and painful blisters to skin. Tens of thousands of Allied and American soldiers who served at the Front had direct experience with one variety or another. When canisters of the gas were fired into Allied lines, whistles or horns were blown to alert all troops to put on their masks immediately. Their officers often reminded them that there were two kinds of soldiers: the quick and the dead. Soldiers who had charge of horses were also expected to put specially made masks on the animals. A delay of just a few seconds could mean hospitalization for weeks. A longer delay could bring permanent blindness, lung damage, or even death. All the men hated the gas masks, which were difficult to adjust properly and restricted one's vision.

The Germans began using gas in 1915 and greatly increased its use in subsequent years. By 1917 Britain and France were producing and using even more gas than Germany, and by 1918 the United States had begun manufacturing large quantities. Official records indicate that about 1.25 million men from both sides of the conflict were gassed, with some 91,000 deaths. More than 50,000 of those killed were Russians on the eastern front; many of those fatalities resulted from a lack of protective masks. By contrast, only about 6,000 British and imperial troops were killed. In 1918 approximately 30 percent of all American battle casualties resulted from mustard gas; of those who wore masks, only about 3 percent died. Official records indicate that nearly 75,000 Americans suffered from gas attacks, with about 1,500 of them dying. In addition to the men listed in official records, there were thousands who were not documented at the time and who, years later, died of gas-related ailments or who suffered from its aftereffects for the remainder of their lives. As will be seen further below, Fred would fall into the latter category.[11]

◆ ◆ ◆

Sept. 23, 1918
France

Dear Mother,

Will drop you a few more lines to let you know I am OK and feeling fine. I wrote you a couple of days ago* from a small village while . . .** then billeted in some farmers barn, which was filled with hay. Now take it from me mother, this bed of hay was the best I have had to sleep on for quiet a long spell, so I th[o]roughly enjoyed myself.

They say we are going to some rest camp for a while but I think it is all B.S. Not that we do not need it because we do need it, as we were at the front for two months. Believe me we are a hard

---

*That letter is missing.

**Fred's letters were written in pencil. Here he erased a line, perhaps because he realized he had given too many specifics regarding his location. The officer censoring his letters would have made him rewrite the entire letter if he included classified information.

looking crew, our clothes all shattered and torn, what we have, part of my equipment I have lost, and I think a little trip to the "cootie" station for a good hot bath, would also help.

The weather over here is very funny this time of year, one day its as hot as blazes, the next it rains, and then turns quiet cold, so a fellow doesnt know what to expect.

The letter I wrote to you a couple of days ago was the first I had written to anyone in about five weeks, so I am a little out of practice, but I dont think it will be for long as I have got an awful lot of correspondance to answer, just as soon as we get to some permanent camp.

You know Harry sent me Charlie Hurds address, and I wrote him. The way he writes he also has had some very good expierance. I certainly would like to see some of the boy's of Co. I.

You can tell Harry that I received snap shots which he sent, that were taken at Cuba lake.* They were all very good with the exception of the two of Celia W & her fellow. I did'nt care much about them although they were fair. The pictures I thought the most of, was my little "sis" Helen. She sure looked fine. In fact always does to me.

You stated that you received my pillow top which I sent a couple of months ago, well mother I am glad that you like it so well. If I get a chance to get any thing that will please you, or the kids, I will send it on. That is about the only good way to spend my money.

I received post card which grandpa Edel had written in French, and was very much surprised to hear from him. So will write him in a few days.

No doubt by the time you get this Harry will have those forms which I signed for my back pay from P.R.R. If you happen to need any money at all use it to your best advantage.

*A resort lake about 17 miles from Olean.

Well mother will have to ring off for now, as I dont know what to write about. Will try and do a little bit better in a couple of day's and send you all a line. Give darling Helen and Harry my love and dont cheat yourself. Also remember me, to May, Martha, and the rest of the neighbors. Give them my best regards.

Also tell "Red" Gabler to drop a line once in a while.

Will close with love
Your loving Son
Fred

◆ ◆ ◆

Almost Hub to Hub

FIGURE 10. Some of the 304th's French 75s Ready to Start the Meuse-Argonne Drive. Reprinted from Howard, *Autobiography of a Regiment*.

On September 24 the 304th Field Artillery arrived at the village of Le Claon near the edge of the dense Argonne forest, 145 miles east of Paris and 25 miles west of Verdun. On September 26 Fred wrote the following in his journal: "Started firing at 2:00 am and fired barrage until 3:00 in the afternoon, believe me some work. But we done our work well as the Hun is retreating. Saw a bunch of Boche prisoners which dough "boys" bring in. We expect to advance guns this pm." September 26 marked the start of the bloodiest battle in United States history, the Meuse-Argonne offensive, which was bordered on the east by the Meuse River and the Argonne Forest on the west. Altogether 1.2 million American soldiers participated in this battle, which raged right up to the signing of the armistice on November 11. The Germans were retreating, but they put up deadly resistance in the thick woods and steep ravines.

The famous story of the 77th Division's "Lost Battalion" occurred during this battle. On October 2, nine infantry companies, consisting of about 554 men, advanced about a half mile further than other units from the Division. As a result, they were trapped by German troops. The Americans put up unflinching resistance, though they were low on food, water, and ammunition. Three hundred fifty of the men were killed or captured over the next week before American dough-boys could rescue the survivors. Thanks to a message transported by a carrier pigeon, the lost battalion could let headquarters know its exact location.

Another celebrated incident from this offensive occurred on October 8. Corporal (later Sergeant) Alvin C. York of the 328th Infantry Regiment in the 82nd Division wiped out a German machine gun nest, killed 15 enemy soldiers, and captured another 132. Despite his lifelong pacifist principles, York was awarded the Medal of Honor and became the most decorated American soldier of the war.

The troops involved in this offensive also included a future President of the United States. Captain Harry S. Truman commanded Battery D, 129th Field Artillery, 60th Brigade, 35th Division.

Fred's journal entry for September 26 was his last. Why did he stop jotting notes in the little book he kept with him? This might be because he was even busier than he had been in previous battles. It might also be because the things he witnessed over the coming weeks were too horrendous for him to put on paper.

Fred had time to write the following three letters because in mid-October the 77th Division was put in reserve for about two weeks when it was relieved by the 78th. The men of the 77th were deloused, allowed time to rest, and given additional training. Fred informs his brother Harry that he has seen all the action any sane man could want. That was as far as the censor would allow regarding specifics. The men in battery F had many close calls and suffered several deaths and injuries from shells and poison gas. Though Fred predicts that the war will soon be over, the fact is that General Pershing and his fellow Allied commanders still thought that the fighting would continue well into 1919. They did not yet realize how depleted Germany and its allies were in men, guns, ammunition, and food.

The relatively inexperienced American troops eventually advanced an average of 34 miles along the line of fighting, killing or wounding more than 100,000 of the enemy, taking 26,000 prisoners, seizing 874 artillery pieces and more than 3,000 machine guns. The 77th Division pushed forward 45 miles, further than any other division, including those of the Regular Army. This American offensive played a decisive role in hastening the end of the war. But it was accomplished at a horrific price. The Meuse-Argonne battle cost the lives of 26,277 American Army soldiers and Marines, with 100,000 others wounded. These numbers were far larger than those of Gettysburg in 1863, Normandy in 1944, or any other battle in American history. During the offensive, Americans employed 2,400 artillery pieces to fire 4 million shells, which represented more than had been fired in the entire Civil War. By the date of the Armistice, the Americans controlled more miles of the Front (83) than did the British (70). The French, aided by Italian and Portuguese divisions, held more than 200 miles.

◆ ◆ ◆

Oct. 13, 1918

Dear Brother,

Received your letter #22, which was dated Sept. 8, and was sure glad to hear from you. Your letter contained quiet a lot of interesting news, so appreciated it, a little bit more than some you write when you are in a hurry to see your girl.

FIGURE 11. 77th Division Doughboys Ready to Advance on Day One of the Meuse-Argonne Drive. Reprinted from *American Armies and Battlefields in Europe*.

So you took a little trip to Warren,* to see Bertha, and got next to another swell little "belle". Well Harry, get a picture from her, and forward some to me, and get my approval. You know I am a pretty fair judge of beauty, and you say she is a peach and real clever. "WATCH YOUR STEP!"

So Otto Wenke received my nice long interesting letter? I tried to make it fair, so I guess I have succeeded. You know when he says a thing, he means it, in pretty near every case. What kind of a job, is student officer, that he is after in the Chicago University, kindly explain?

So Mr Mason was called back from New York to await the draft. Well kid I dont think he will pass. I should say he would be doing more for his country in directing Railroads, than in doing YMCA work.

So you are going to have sister start in music from Prof Hill? Well she will certainly have to do her bit and practice, or otherwise it will be a waste of money, because Hill is pretty steep in his tuition. Tell her every time she starts to practice to think of her brother in France, doing his bit, so she had ought to do her's, and be able to make that piano talk by the time I get ready to come home.

I have been receiving the Olean Times, at "times" but they are from two to three months old when I get them, they are what I would call ancient history, but welcome just the same. The last bunch I received a couple of days ago were dated from Aug. 10th up.

Harry, havent you received those slips, so you could get my back pay? I sent them, in the next out going mail, so they ought to be their by this time. Kindly let me know the total amount of back pay which I have coming? You spoke about going to Havens to see the

*Pennsylvania town about 65 miles from Olean.

photo play "Four years in Germany."* I think I saw this production while I was still an inmate of Camp Upton. It sure was good.

You certainly are commanding a pretty fair salary for a boy if you keep on, you might work yourself up to a M.M.** like old "Cascaret" Selby. You know you never can tell.

So Gen [evieve?] Provins is moving back to Olean? (Gods country) I would like to see her again, and would also like to have you tell her, to drop a few lines.

Take it from me Albert Fagan took quiet a chance, in sending [the] letter which you said was so interesting. The "dough boys" (infantry) take quiet a lot of chance in this game than the artillery, although we have seen, all the action, any sane man would want to go through. We have been shelled extensively which is a common occurance, bombed by aeroplanes, been in gas attacks, machine gun fire, in fact everything that goes in this war game, except going over the top. So I think you had better wait until I get home, which I dont think is so very far off, and I'll tell you some pretty fair expierances, which I have gone through.

From the looks of things this war will not last over a month, so you will not have to make up a Xmas box for me. Thats what I call a pretty good hint eh what? Well bud will have to close for this time, so give my love to Mother and Sister, and the rest of my friends.

Your loving brother
Fred

P.S. Will try to write in a day or so, that is, if I have time.

---

*A 1918 motion picture about the experiences of a U.S. ambassador in Germany.
**Master Machinist.

◆ ◆ ◆

The letter below shows that Fred continued to say his prayers and, when possible, attend church services. Like all others in his family, he was a practicing Catholic. His hometown of Olean had many Catholic immigrants of Irish, Italian, German, and Lebanese descent.

◆ ◆ ◆

Oct. 14, 1918
France

Dearest Mother

Received your letter dated Sept. 10 and was very glad to hear from you also glad to hear that every one is well and in good health. This is what counts most with me.

I sent a few pictures of myself a week or so ago so you can see that I am in very good health, and not losing an ounce of weight.

You wanted to know if I had to stand guard. Of course every body does both day and night, this is nothing at all to worry about.

I was very glad to hear that Christie Gabler got exempted because the army is no place for him, but he got a nice little trip out of it any how. But about his shyness, he would of got over that soon enough. Give him my congradulations.

So Irene Ellis has a baby girl, well thats very good news. Ask her if she wants a good nurse maid. If she does will try and get back as soon as possible.

Believe me mother if you have bought a new stove, I will be home sure to bake my shins up against it. Especially because its all in the game.

As I have written before I am on the guns, and like it very much. Believe me we certainly give the Huns a little reception every time we open fire. From the looks of things over here mother, I dont think this war will keep up very long, because its all we hear is pease talk. Believe me it can not come any to quick for me, because I certainly would hate to put a winter in over on this side.

Now about writing, I write most every time I get a chance, which is not very often, but will try to do a little bit better in the future. You know I get quite a lot of mail and I try to answer all of them. Received a $5.00 money order from the old gent the other day, but dont know where I can spend it.

We have been at the front for over 100 day's, so expect to go to some rest camp, with in a very short time.

The weather over hear is getting to be a little chilly but I suppose its the same in the states.

Now about that allotment I will try and find out what I can do about it. You ought to have written about it before. If Mrs. Ringbauer gets $5.00 extra for Theresa, you ought to be entitled to the same for Helen.*

On Sunday's after I come from church. Another thing you asked me if I still say my prayers. This is something I never would forget. I go to confession and communion as often as I can, but havent been to church in two months. The chaplins come around once in a while to hear our confessions, so this is better than not going at all. Sunday is just like any other day in the army, we have got our work to do, and its got to be done, no laying off for nothing. Cheer up mother it wont be for always.

---

*One can infer from this letter that the government was sending Fred's mother the regular monthly allotment of $15 as compensation for the fact that the family's main wage earner (Fred) was in the Army. Given the fact that the war would soon be over, it is doubtful that an extra $5.00 was approved.

Received a bunch of Olean papers last night with my Mooseheart magazine. This latter is sure some treat. Well dearest mother will close for now with love and best wishes for all.

Your beloved son
Fred.

P.S. Will enclose a few photos. Give May L and Martha Gross one, as they asked for a picture. There is two of each. I sent a couple to the old gent also. Give my best regards to the Ellis's and give them my congradulations. Also give the neighbours my best.

FIGURE 12. Rain and Mud Were Constant Companions Through the Fall of 1918. Reprinted from Howard, *Autobiography of a Regiment*.

♦ ♦ ♦

Fred wrote the following letter as the 304th F.A. was about to be relieved and spend several days billeted in a village called Four de Paris.

♦ ♦ ♦

Oct. 17, 1918

Dearest Mother,

Just a few lines, as I havent much time to write, a very long letter. I am writing this in regards to the Christmas Package coupon, which entitles every soldier to his Xmas present. You must follow directions very closely and not put in any more than three pounds. Now about what I would like put in as much chocalate (Hershey chocalate bars prefered) as you can, a few sticks of peanut candy if you can crowd them in, and - - - - - well I guess I had better quite because I think I am way over the limit now. This isnt much of a present, but its a lot better than none at all. I am well and feeling in the best of spirits today, because I think we are going to get relieved, from the front for a while at least. So I guess its the lousing station, and then a nice, much earned rest for a couple of weeks at least. Love to all.

> Your loving Son
> Fred
> Bugler F.A. Kittleman
> Btry F 304th FA
> Amex Forces via N.Y.

P.S. Do not delay about sending this package. The sooner I get it the better.

Fred

♦ ♦ ♦

Oct 21, 1918

Dearest Mother,

Received your letter which was dated Sept 26, and will answer immediately. I am well and feeling "Boo-Koo" very well in Francaise.

You ask me if I have been in battle? Yes mother I have been battling away for the last three months, but am now on my way to a rest camp. We left the front the other day, to get deloused. This consists of getting a good hot shower bath. (The first warm bath I have had in pretty near 3 months) also a new bunch of clothes. The men all receive new under clothes, socks, new suit, in fact every thing is new, and it makes a fellow feel 10 yrs younger.

Now there is one thing I want you to do, and that is, to stop worrying about me, because I am OK. Just because Ernest Dubler was wounded, is no sign you should get all excited. I could have told you a month ago, if it wasn't for the censoring of the letters. I know how you are, so why make you feel worse than you really do.

Now about Harry's case you want to try and try hard, because you need that kids support. Now if he was taken away, you would be what we call "Out of luck". Cheer up mother, and keep a good stiff upper lip, because there are better days acoming for all of us. That is, if it is Gods will. Let us pray and hope for the best anyhow.*

---

*In August 1918 the federal government amended the Selective Service Act to expand the pool of men eligible for the draft to all aged 18 to 45. As things turned out, Harry was not called up. No doubt this was mostly because the war ended sooner than expected.

You ask me if I have written to your aunt in France? No because I cant get anyone to write French for me. Have Grandpa Edel write a French letter telling about me etc. and enclose it in one of your letters and I will send it to her. Also put her address on it as I have lost the other one you sent me.

So Ed Finger does not like army life eh? Well wait until he gets to France he will get a real taste of it. He will find out that when he left the old army barracks in the states. He left a home.

Now about that Christmas box. I have sent you a Xmas package slip, in a previous letter, and if you havent shipped the box away yet, I would like to have you enclose that big Waltham (silver) watch the one the old gent gave me. Be sure and pack this very securely so it does not break. This is something I am badly in need of as I broke my wrist watch. I have also thought of another thing. A good jack knife (with a couple of good blades, can opener, cork screw etc all in one). This is also very handy. The rest of the space fill in with chocalate. Well Mother will close with love and kisses for all.

Your loving Son
Fred

P.S. I had to fill the last few lines in, by candle light. Its just about 6:00 pm and its dark as blazes. I received a bunch of Olean Times, this evening so will try reading for a while.

The rest for Helen the girl wonder, with the million dollar smile. I received her letter yesterday and such a line of bull, why, I dont believe I could spread it any better. And the way she describes her English teacher. Gee! she must be a "pippin"* "<u>the big cow</u>".

---

*A highly admired person.

And Mother! I think you had better watch your daughter, or Mrs Hartweg will have a new addition to her family table. Of course you would'nt be losing very much, but just think of the loss Mrs H. would suffer. So kindly look into this matter mother dear, and advise me of the result. Hoping to get an immeadiate reply.

I remain
Your loving son
Fred

P.S. Give all the neighbours my best, and inform Harry that I will answer his letter within a few day's.

Tired, Dirty, Ragged, and Lousy

FIGURE 13. The Condition of Most Soldiers When the War Ended. Reprinted from Howard, *Autobiography of a Regiment*.

P.S. Dont forget watch and knife.

Bugler F.A. Kittleman
304th F.A. Btry F
Amex Forces via N.Y.

◆ ◆ ◆

Fred's hometown newspapers occasionally published letters that some of the Olean men who served in the 304th Field Artillery had written to their families. Below are extracts from a letter from Private Frank R. Jordan. Like Fred, Jordan spares his family from the bloody details of what he was experiencing.

◆ ◆ ◆

France, Oct. 31, 1918

Dear Mother, Brother and Sister:

Just a line to let you know I am well, along with the boys from home town.

We are doing our part in this war and doing it with a smile that the Huns cant take off. We have seen a lot of fighting and hard at that, but it is making the Huns go back to the land where they came from and you don't know how happy we are when we are told to move ahead.

I have seen France from one end to the other and will have a lot to tell on my return.

We do not have lights at night because the Huns would see it and shell us; sometimes we can fix our dug-out so we can have a light and in it and smoke.

The K. of C. is at the front with us and we can get things from them and it does not cost anything; also the Red Cross does good work. They give us lots of things, so tell the people to help them all they can because it is helping to win the war. What you do for them you do for us.

I will close sending my love to you all and hope you will not worry about me, as God will take care of us and will return as many boys to their mothers and wives and friends as he can.

With love,
Pvt. Frank R. Jordan
Headquarters Co.
304th F. A.[12]

◆ ◆ ◆

Rumors of peace talks had been flying up and down the front lines for weeks in October and early November. But heavy fighting continued in the Meuse-Argonne sector. In fact it was in this period that Fred and his buddies in the 304th Field Artillery experienced their worst days. Of course, Fred avoided revealing any of this to his family. No letter from him survives between October 21 and November 25. The wording in the letter below suggests that he wrote none during these weeks. One reason was lack of time. Fred's unit was working non-stop, moving its heavy guns through muddy, shell-scarred terrain in order to maintain pressure on the retreating Germans. There was also another reason. On October 28 German gas canisters landed amidst the men working the French 75s in Batttery F. Years later John P. Clarke, who was working on the same gun crew as Fred, wrote the following:

> A number of men in our detail were "diggin-in" the guns when we were all strickened with gas. Among the men I remember on the detail were Willis Dever, Wm. C. Matter, Jr, Jim McManus, Fredrick Kittleman and several others. Dever, Matter, myself and a few others returned to receive hospital treatment which lasted about a week. At the time I did not know where McManus and Kittleman went after we were nipped with the gas, but I later learned that they stayed with the guns and had continued to "move up" while we were in the hospital.

William C. Matter likewise recalled that day years later:

> All [the others] were sent to the hospital with the exception of Kittleman and McManus. These men were sent back to man the guns by Captain Eberstadt, who was our commanding officer at the time, when they too should have been sent to the hospital. . . . after being discharged from the hospital . . . [I] returned to . . . [the] battery and found Frederick Kittleman to be in a sickly condition and unable to hold his own as before. . . . Frederick Kittleman was continually going to the doctor regarding his being gassed.

Clarke's and Matter's affidavits of 1934 are included in the papers now in the possession of Fred's grandson Robert Deckman. The fact that Fred stayed at his gun despite his suffering certainly marked him as a brave, uncomplaining soldier. However, the fact that he was not admitted to a hospital at that time would later cause problems for him. More on this in the Epilogue.

The armistice ending the fighting was signed in a French railway car in Compiègne on the morning of November 11. Four horrifying years of the worst bloodbath that the world had yet seen finally came to an end. Why did Fred not write to his family until two weeks later? His mother, brother, and sister must have been frantic, as American newspapers gave graphic reports of the staggering losses in the Meuse-Argonne offensive.

Part of the explanation could be that Fred was still suffering from the poison gas, perhaps with headaches and poor vision. Another explanation is that Fred's regiment received no rest in the days following the armistice. On November 12 Battery F and other batteries in its brigade were relieved by a French battalion. Fred and his fellow soldiers then began a long march southward, away from the front. The 304th Field Artillery had been through hell and merited the jubilant thanks showered on the men by French villagers who thronged their route over the next several days. The soldiers in the French battalion must have been envious. For them, the war had lasted four years, and yet they had to remain at the front to ensure that the peace would be maintained. The 304th was also fortunate in that none of its men were assigned to the U.S. army of occupation that would remain in German territory for the foreseeable future. The 304th did, however, turn over nearly all of its horses to the unfortunate artillery units that had to remain. The final American troops were not brought home until 1923.

Fred wrote the following letter from the village of Briquenay, in the Ardennes region, about 140 miles northeast of Paris. There the 304th rested several days and enjoyed a sumptuous Thanksgiving Day meal.

◆ ◆ ◆

Nov. 25, 1918

Dear Mother,

Will drop a few lines, to let you know I am well, and outside of a little cold, in the finest of health, and expect to be home very soon, probably before this letter reaches you. Hears hoping.

Believe me mother I am very glad that "big show" is over, as I was getting very much disgusted with the life of knocking about, the way we were going, when the Huns started retreating. We were always on the go and this is no fun.

As soon as I get home you will receive a full account of my expierances in "Sunny France".

I'll bet their were some very joyous people on that side, when the news came over the wires that the Germans wanted an armistice. I can just imagine the sensation it created.

Well mother will drop off writing, as I have to go out to drill in about five minutes. Hoping this letter finds you and the rest in the best of health.

Your loving Son
Fred
Bugler F.A. Kittleman
Btry. F 304th F.A.
Amex Forces A.E.F.

◆ ◆ ◆

On December 2 the 304th Field Artillery boarded a train and traveled to an area in the Aube River valley, about 175 miles southeast of Paris. Half of the regiment, including Battery F, was billeted in the village of Aubepierre-sur-Aube, while the other half was about three miles away in Lignerolles. Despite unending rumors about imminent departure for America, the 304th was to remain billeted there in barns, private homes, and makeshift barracks until February 8.

There were two million American soldiers in France and simply not enough ships to carry all of them home immediately. Other problems also presented themselves, including finding temporary billets for them, caring for the tens of thousands who were sick or wounded, and deciding which units needed to remain for the army of occupation.

Even though the war was over, Fred's letters still had to be read and signed by an officer. Nonetheless, he was now allowed to reveal his location and provide many other particulars that would have been forbidden earlier.

Fred's sister gave this letter to one of the local newspapers, the *Olean Evening Herald*, which reprinted it on January 8, 1919.

◆ ◆ ◆

Aubepierre, France
Dec. 8, 1918

Dear Sister:

I am well and in the best of health and longing very much for the time when Uncle Sam sees fit to send us boys back home again. From the looks of things it might be a month and possibly two months. A person can never tell as orders change very suddenly in the army. For a while it was rumored the 77th would be home for Xmas, but this all went up in smoke. It sure would be a wonderful Xmas for all of us if we could only be home.

Cheer up Sis, there are better days for you and I.

I am very glad you received the photos. The group picture which you spoke about was pretty fair. One of the fellows was an Olean boy, James McManus; the other two New York boys.

I was very sorry to learn that my old pal, Ambrose H[arvey], died. He sure was one fine chum and I will miss him more than once when I get back; too bad!

Well, Sister, will have to close as it's getting late. With love and best wishes for a Merry Xmas for all.

Your loving brother
Fred

FIGURE 14. James McManus and Fred. Fred's gas mask is hanging in its case by his side. Courtesy of Robert Deckman.

◆ ◆ ◆

In the letter below Fred gives his brother Harry a detailed account of all the fighting he saw in the summer and fall of 1918. Whereas the first years of war on the Western Front had been marked by trenches and virtual stalemate, the war had become one of movement by the time that American forces became actively involved. Fred notes that in the final weeks of the conflict the Germans were retreating so fast that the Americans had trouble keeping up with them. Muddy roads, the slow and awkward movement of teams of horses pulling large wagons or artillery pieces, and the sheer magnitude of hundreds of thousands of troops converging on the same locations created almost impenetrable traffic jams.[13]

◆ ◆ ◆

Aubepierre
December 12, 1918

Dear Brother

I just had quiet a job sorting my mail, that is old mail from new, and I find that you have done your share so will write to you first of all. The last letter you wrote #36 was written in front of "our" little stove in the parlor, well kid I got something on you this time. I am writing this letter in an old mans house which is quiet near my billet. He is a wonderful man in fact, reminds me very much like grandpa Edel. He is about the same age, and just as talkative when he gets "half shot." The only trouble he keeps on chewing the rag in French, and my French vocabulary is very limited, so every thing he says, I say oui (we, meaning yes). In this way we get along in pretty good shape.

Well Harry you wanted to know about the last drive, well I will give you a very brief history of the whole game since I have been in it. We first went into action on the Lorraine front at a place called Petonville about 8 or 10 kilo from Bacarat. We arrived here on July 13 from Camp De Souge. near Bordeaux. We left this front Aug 1st for action on the Chateau Thierry front, and on the Vesle River, where the Germans made a stand. Here the Germans made it very lively for some time and finally after very desperate fighting, especially for the infantry and engineers, we dislodged them from the mountain overlooking the Vesle River. The Germans loosing very heavily started to retreat. We finally drove them across the Aisne river. We were then relieved by the Italian troops on Sept 13. We were then located in front of a village called Pearls [Perles], about three Kilo from the famous city of Fismes. On Sept 14th we started for another front. We arrived at a village called Le Claon 8 or 10 Kilo from St Menhould [Sainte Menehould] on Sept 23, just in time for the famous Argonne drive. On Sept 26 at 2:00 am we started to fire, and kept it up until 3:30 pm. Each gun firing around 780 shells 14 guns to a battery. Believe me the Germans sure got hell. From there we advanced every day capturing village after village, until the Germans made a stand near the village of Fliaville [Fléville] about Oct 24.

It was a bitter fight, and we saw quiet a few hardships, but it was worth it. We then had a few day's rest and started the final drive on Nov 1. Well Harry I cannot find words enough to tell you of the barrage which the Americans put over on the Germans. Their were hundreds of guns from the 37 MM (1 pounders) up to the big naval guns in the rear.* The Hun sure thought he was in hell when they started to send these iron rations over to him, so doing the next best

---

*The huge naval guns were mounted on railway cars. They could hurl 1400-pound projectiles 25 miles into the rear of the German lines.

thing he started to run, which made it very difficult for us to keep in touch with him. We finally ended up above a village called Raucourt 6 or 8 Kilo from Sedan. It certainly was pretty tough for all concerned, as we advanced so fast that the quarter master corps had great difficulty in bringing up food supplies owing to roads being mined, and the amount of traffic on the roads. Luckily the Germans had great fields of cabbage, and beet sugar this solved our food problem to a certain extent.* Thanks to the Mess sergeant, who fixed it up for us. Well Bud taking everything in consideration I feel as good as ever, and very glad I was over here to participate in the war because it was one great expierance if one came out of it OK.

And when the news of Armistice came to suspend firing we took it very calmly because we did not have very much faith in it, but this time it was straight goods. It seemed very funny for the first few nights hearing no firing, but we soon got used to it again and got all caught up with our sleep, which we needed badly. After two weeks time the French relieved us, and we moved until we arrived on the other side of Grandpre, a railroad centre and from their traveled until we came to our present location Aubepierre. We expect to remain in this village some time. Well brother think I have wrote enough so will close with plenty of love for all.

> Your loving brother
> Fred
> Bugler F.A. Kittleman
> Btry F 304th F.A.
> Amex Forces

---

*The battle lines in this sector had remained so stable for four years that the Germans not only planted crops but fixed up some of their shelters with all the comforts of home.

With best wishes for a Merry Xmas and a happy new year to all. Very sorry I can not participate in these, am unavoidably detained.

Your loving brother
Fred

P.S. Will write to Helen and Mother later. Give my love to May and all the neighbours my best regards.

◆ ◆ ◆

Aubepierre
Dec. 15, 1918

Dear Mother and Sister,

Received your most welcome letters a couple of days ago, but just [now] find time in which to answer. I also received your Xmas cards, which I appreciate very much especially the one in which your picture was enclosed. This was real nice. Last but not least I want to thank each, for your kindness in sending money orders. It came at just the right time because I was nearly broke. Enough said.

From the way you people write Olean sure done its share of celebrating when the great news flashed over the wires that hostilities had ceased, as for us soldiers, we took it very calmly, because we did not put very much stock in it, because we heard to many rumors, about peace being signed, Germans given an armistice etc. Gee! but the army is one big game to get used to.

The only troublesome part of the whole game is the cooties. At times they drive a man almost insane. Every night before bed time five or six fellows will gather around a candle, and proceed to delouse himself. Its very amusing at times to hear the different remarks each fellow makes after he gets from 25 up.

Well mother I wish I were able to be home with you for Xmas, but its out of the question. So we will have to make the best of it.

Well as I am not in much of a mood for letter writing will have to close until some future date. With love and best wishes for a joyful Xmas.

Your loving son and brother
Fred
Bugler F.A. Kittleman
Btry F. 304th F.A.
Amex Forces

◆ ◆ ◆

In the letter below Fred writes that he does not know what to write about. It is curious that he does not choose to mention the events of a couple of weeks earlier. Sometime shortly before December 25, the 304th Field Artillery and other units from the 77th Division boarded a train and travelled about 200 miles to the town of Humes in the Haute-Marne department northeast of Paris. It was there, on Christmas Day, that General Pershing and President Wilson, the latter recently arrived in France, reviewed some 10,000 troops in a huge wheat field. Fred and the other men in the 304th Field Artillery were given the privilege of giving the President a 21-gun salute.[14]

◆ ◆ ◆

January 6, 1919
Aubepierre

Dear brother:

Received your letter #41 dated Dec 12th, it sure contained a very good amount of interesting topics. I really don't know what to write about but probably will think of something as I go along.

Yesterday being a very nice day, three of us started out to see the cascades, or water falls which are situated five kilometers from this village. It certainly is a very pretty sight. The source of this water fall is nothing but a little brook, about two feet wide, but nature sure done it's work well.

Poor Mrs. Fadel is certainly having a terrible time with her foot. I think if she would of had it amputated when the doctors told her to she would of eliminated a lot of suffering. Give her my best regards, and tell her I wish her all kinds of luck.

Received a check from the First National [Bank] to the tune of five bucks, and understand that the Exchange is now sending ten. Their must be quiet a bit of rivalry between these banks, so I hope that the Olean Trust comes in the race, and sends on fifteen or twenty. You know Harry money is allways welcome.*

So Lena H. is the mother of a nice little baby. Tell me bud, does it look anything like its mother, if so, its enough said.

How about Mike Woods is he still on the job?

Now about "Stub" Becker that kid is a regular "imp" of the devil, so your news didnt surprise me one bit, because he was allways getting in "dutch." Give him my best.

---

*The banks in Olean were sending monetary gifts to thank local men who had served their country.

Before I forget, you asked me to send you a ring but this is quiet impossible, as I am afraid to take a chance on the mail. So just keep your shirt on, and wait until I get home, then you shall have your ring. Ask Helen what she wrote to me regarding this ring question, it sure was "hot stuff."

Well brother I think I have written enough trash for one night so will ring off.

With plenty of love for all

Your bother
Fred
Bugler F.A. Kittleman
Btry F. 304th F.A.
Amex Forces

◆ ◆ ◆

Aubepierre Francaise
Jan. 20 1919

Dear Brother,
Received three letters from you last Saturday (Dec 19, Dec 24, & Dec 29) and in all three you state you have not been receiving any mail from me. You stated that Nov 14 was the last you have heard of me. There must be something wrong somewhere, because I have been writing quite often. Its been the same way over here, your letters were the first I had received in over a month.

You wanted to know if I have been to "gay Paree." Gee kid I wish they would give me a chance.

Some of the men, sgts. & corpls, have been on pass but I do not think any more passes will be issued as we are slated to go home very shortly. I think I would rather tour the states anyhow.

And speaking about the growler,* I would give anything to wet my whistle on one again, but from what I understand the states are going dry, so there is not much hopes, thanks to the W.C.T.U. (Whiskey Can't Touch Us).

The news about Geo Bremer came as quiet a surprise as I didn't know he had a divorce from Hazel. Tell him I wish him better luck than last time. He has a very good taste when it comes to women.

We have been having some very fine weather. Its <u>almost</u> warm enough to go around in your shirt sleeves.

Well bud will have to close. The soldiers in my billet are making so much noise I cannot write (never could).

Love to all.

> Fred
> Bugler F.A. Kittleman
> Btry F, 304th F.A.
> Amex Forces

◆ ◆ ◆

Howard's regimental history plus numerous other books on the AEF note how bored and discontented the soldiers became during the months when they awaited shipment back to the states. To keep the men occupied, the army forced them to drill every morning.

---

*A pitcher of beer.

According to their specialties, the men also had to take additional training in areas like map reading, radio and telephone operation, and even equitation (a small number of horses had been acquired for the purpose). In Fred's case, there was bugle school. All the men grumbled at these forced activities, as they saw no purpose to them now that the war was over. A few soldiers also took optional classes in academic subjects like French, arithmetic, and history. All the men enjoyed the afternoon games of baseball, basketball, and football. They also organized track meets and played tug-of-war. The soldiers also entertained themselves in ways that seem quaint in today's age of television and the Internet. They sang in glee clubs, played in bands, put on vaudeville shows, and even organized a medieval pageant. The 304th's Regimental Association in New York sent them money to obtain musical instruments, Christmas turkeys, and cigarettes. The men purchased hundreds of Christmas gifts for the children in the two villages. The staff photographers in the signal corps were also kept busy filming these events, and some of these silent movies can be seen today on YouTube.[15]

◆ ◆ ◆

Jan 27 1919
Aubepierre France

Dearest Mother,

I have just returned from bugle school, so will write a few lines to you before dinner.

Yesterday was a big day for me, as I received "Beauko" mail, so I have quite a job on my hands in answering mail, and as usual yours always comes first.

Last night about 8 or 9 o'clock it started to snow a little, and imagine my surprise this morning after getting up (6:45 first call) to find mother earth covered with about three or four inches of snow. It sure made me feel at home. This has been the first snow I have seen since being in France. It would do me a lot of good to see our dear son and brother Harry on the job with a snow shovel and grumbling as usual. Gee but I bet he misses me now.

Received the pictures of Helen and Theresa in one of Harry's letters. They certainly are fine.

I hardly knew my little sister, as she seems to be quite a lot taller, in fact looks every inch a lady. I do not like to hand out compliments, but really think she deserves one. Mother you certainly can be proud of her. I know I am. This will no doubt give her a little swelled head. Iskabible.

Mother you asked me, as a personal favor to Mrs. Harvey to find out where Ambrose is buried, also if possible to have pictures taken of grave. I will find out this very night and do all in my power to get results. Our division is expected to move this week so I cannot guarantee an answer, but will try my very best. Ambrose was a fellow whom I very often think about, as he was one of my very best friends, so tell his mother I will do my best.

Well mother think I have written enough for this time, so will close. Love to all.

Your loving son
Fred

Give my best to all the neighbours.

Mother I sent you a copy of the Stars and Stripes last night. Its quite an interesting paper.*

Bugler F.A. Kittleman
Btry F 304th F.A.
Amex Forces

◆ ◆ ◆

On February 8 the 304th boarded trains and made the long trip westward to an area about 215 miles southwest of Paris. Battery F was billeted in the town of Fercé, while other units were scattered in nearby towns and villages. The trip was miserable. The men were

FIGURE 15. The Medieval Pageant Organized by the Bored Troops. Reprinted from Howard, *Autobiography of a Regiment*.

Stars and Stripes is a government-funded newspaper whose main readers are members of the U.S. armed services serving abroad. During World War I it appeared weekly. Its editor was Harold Ross, who later would found *The New Yorker* magazine. Today it appears daily in both print and electronic formats.

packed into the notorious French freight cars called "Hommes 40, Chevaux 8," which meant they could carry 40 men or 8 horses. The weather was bitterly cold. If the men sought ventilation, they froze. But keeping the doors shut meant that in the smelly, dusty compartments they coughed and sneezed on each other through the journey. Many developed influenza or pneumonia, with several dying.

◆ ◆ ◆

Ferce France
Feb 12 1919

Dear sister,

Will drop you a few lines to let you know that you are not forgotten. I must tell you about the trip which I have just completed. We left Aubepierre 8:00 am Feb 8, walked 15 kilo, with full packs, arrived at La Tracy [Latrécy] (the rail head) at about 12:00 n[oon]. Believe me sis it was quite cold. We boarded our side door pullmans at about 4:00 pm. If you have ever read Empeys "First Call" you will get a very good idea of what traveling is in these famous French 40-8's (40 men or 8 horses).* We then traveled 3 nights and 2 days, arriving in Ferce yesterday morning about 6:00 am. This place (just as bad as the name) is about 23 kilo from Le Mans.**

I think our next stop will be the embarkation port, so do not think it will be a great while before I am homeward bound.

Well sis, this is about all the news I have for this time. Will think of a little more later, and drop Harry a line.

---

*Arthur Guy Empey's book *First Call: Guide Posts to Berlin* was published in 1918. It is not likely that Helen would have had access to such a book.

**Actually, Fercé is about 160 kilometers (100 miles) southwest of Le Mans.

I am writing this letter in the guard-house. We have to stand bugle guard for 24 hrs every once in a while.

Well "butch" will close with love and kisses for all.

Your affectionate brother
Fred

P.S. Give the neighbours my best regards.

Bugler F.A. Kittleman
304th F.A. Btry F.
Amex Forces.

◆ ◆ ◆

" Hommies Forty "

Figure 16. One of the French 40-Man, 8-Horse Freight Cars. Reprinted from Howard, *Autobiography of a Regiment.*

In the letter below, Fred lets his mother know that he is in a hospital but tells her this is merely a precaution to make sure that he has not contracted influenza. Just as he concealed from his family the fact that he had been gassed twice, now he hides the fact that indeed he was very sick with influenza as well as with possible aftereffects from mustard gas. One of his Battery F fellow soldiers, Peter Koenig, later recalled that Fred was in the hospital for about two weeks and was "a very sick man."[16]

This strain of influenza came to be called Spanish flu, and the epidemic it created formed one of the most deadly worldwide demographic catastrophes of modern times. This particularly deadly strain of influenza attained the nickname "Spanish" because of early reports of its spread throughout that country. In actuality, however, there is no agreement about its source. There were early outbreaks of it in widely dispersed parts of the world, including in the state of Kansas.

Persons who contracted it often came down with pneumonia, which greatly lessened their chances of surviving. From the fall of 1918 to the summer of 1919 some 675,000 people in the United States died from it—more than all the American combat fatalities in World War I, World War II, Korea, and Vietnam combined. The contagion caused between 50 and 100 million fatalities worldwide. There was no known cure. Physicians at the time thought it was caused by bacteria; only in the 1930s did researchers determine that it was a virus. Thousands of American soldiers died of it while in training camps in America or on board ships taking them to France. In the early months of 1918 the epidemic spread to Allied and German soldiers in the trenches. Indeed, rather than admitting that his own flawed strategies were at fault, German Commander Erich von Ludendorff blamed the flu for the failure of his army's spring offensives in that year. The men of the 304th Field Artillery must have considered themselves fortunate to have escaped the illness, until it hit them with a vengeance just when they were hoping to go home. Nearly half of the men in Battery F came down with it. Altogether nearly 47,000 American soldiers (those in camps in the United States plus those in France) died from the flu or pneumonia, which nearly equaled the total number of American combat deaths. Of the two million men in the AEF in France, nearly 400,000 were stricken with influenza. Given the enormity of this epidemic on both sides of the Atlantic, Fred was wise not to worry his family by telling them the truth.

◆ ◆ ◆

Feb 16 1919

Dear Mother,

A few lines to let you know what I am doing. Just at present I am in a French Hospital feeling in the best of health. Nothing the matter as far as I can see. The reason I am here is because the influenza is starting to raise cain, so all men who have a temperature of 99° or over. Its the hospital. I came here yesterday morning and could of left this afternoon but white sheets on a nice little bed appeal strongly to me, so will make one more night of it. The meals here is another pretty good feature, as its very good. First of all you will receive meat broth with plenty of bread. Next comes creamed potatoes with a very good portion of pork, or roast beef. Then rice pudding. We also get pretty near a quart of milk, each meal, besides tea or coffee. Then to wash this down a big cup, which also holds pretty near a quart, of vin rouge. Gee mother its a great life.

Our battery which is composed of about 188 men, of these about 90 are in the hospital. The 77th Division is scheduled to sail Mar

5th, so the medical men are taking no chances, to have an epidemic of influenza raging in the division. This would, no doubt, keep us over here some time.

The hospital is situated about twenty-five kilos from Ferce.

Well mother will have to close for now as I am running out of ammunition.

> With loads of love
> Fred
> Bugler F.A. Kittleman
> 304th F.A. Btry F
> Amex Forces

◆ ◆ ◆

Ferce Feb 19 1919

Dear Mother,

A few lines to let you know I am well, and back to the battery again. I wrote you in a previous letter that I was in a Francaise Croix Rouge Hospital. One thing I got was a very good rest, something which all the boys in the A.E.F. need.

I received your cards, a letter from Helen, and the bundle of Collier magazines, and the Olean Times, which I appreciated very much. I also received a letter from Madame Eliza Dozol, but cannot find anyone to translate it for me. As soon as I can dope out the contents of her letter, will write to her.* Also received a letter from

---

*She was probably a friend or relative of the Edel family in Alsace.

Fred Christopher of Falconer, together with a few newspaper clippings and a check for 5 beans. Am having a wonderful time. He states work is quiet slow so he is again going to migrate to Okla, to get a job in the oil fields. That lad sure is some globe trotter.

The dope which Helen had in her letter about the 77th Div. sailing March 5 was the same we had, but it seems now as if we were set back until around April 1. We might be home April 1, 1920. Who knows?

Well mother havent any news so will close.

Your loving son
Fred

Am sending you a few views of the church connected with the hospital. This hospital before the war was a big French monastery. It's a very nice place!!. Eleven views in all.

Bugler F.A. Kittleman
Btry F 304th F.A.
Amex Forces

◆ ◆ ◆

Feb 23 1919
Ferce, France

Dear sister Helen,
As the weather is very bad today, will devote my time to writing a few letters, of which I have many.

FIGURE 17. Fred's Sister Helen, 1920s. Courtesy of Lois Zach.

Went to church this morning, for the first time in three weeks. No so bad for me, eh? One good thing about army life, going to church is not compulsory, so if a fellow cares to take a little nap, why no one will bother him, so I think I had better re-enlist. What do you say? Ah oui.

Before I forget, you wrote me and said, you got all you school exams but one and Harry sends me a letter which I received yesterday, and contradicts your statements. I do not know who is at fault, but if you are, you're going to get a thrashing when I get home, and a good one at that.

Now for a little prose, you might like it.

TO HELEN
Helen, thy beauty is to me
Like those Nicean barks of your,
That gently, o'er a perfumed sea,
The weary way worn wanderer bore
To his own native shore
In desperate seas long wont to roam
Thy hyacinths hair, thy classic face,
Thy Naiad airs have brought me home
To the glory that was Greece
And the grandeur that was Rome

Lo! In you brilliant window niche
How statue like I see thee stand
The agate lamp within thy hand!
Oh. Psyche, from the regions which
Are Holy Land!

This poem, written by Edgar Allen Poe sure does fit you to a T.*

---

*Fred must have found this poem in a book he borrowed from the Y.M.C.A. or one of the other service organizations. In copying the poem into his letter he made a couple of errors. For example, in line two "barks of your" should be "barks of yore."

Now that you have my sentiments, what do you think of me? A d---- fool. Oh I thought so.

Well sis I have written enough trash so will have to ring off until some other time. Hoping to see you real soon. I remain your loving brother.

Fred
Bugler F.A. Kittleman
Btry F 304th F.A.
Amex Forces

FIGURE 18. Fred's Brother Harry in 1920, shortly before his death. Courtesy of Lois Zach.

◆ ◆ ◆

Ferce
Feb 25 1919

Dear brother,

Will drop you a few more lines to let you know I am still kicking. I am in the very best of health and hope that this letter will find you all the same.

I understand that the Spanish Influenza is starting up again, so be very carefull, and use every precaution so you do not contract it.

Its been raining nearly all day long, so its all I've done is to hug the fire. (I'm sorry it isn't "little" Mary, from N. Olean).

Well, bud, I wrote you in a previous letter that we were to be reviewed by Genl. Pershing.* Well it came off yesterday. It was one wonderfull sight to see the whole division, between 30,000 to 40,000 men. Genl. Pershing was very well pleased and stated that the 77th Div. was one of the very best in France, and would go home very soon. Just at present, in the states, the 27th Division has received quiet a name, which they justly deserve, but wait until the "Fighting 77th" gets back. Boy if any division ever went through hell, it was ours. Read the newspapers and find out for yourselves.

Received your letter of Feb. 7th, and as Helen would say, it was a very "stingy" one. If what you say is true about everything being so high, why I think I had better let Uncle Sam keep me.** Now

---

*That letter is missing.

**Here Fred refers to the inflation of prices that took place in the United States during the war. The Federal Reserve System had been created in 1913. Thanks to that, the government could put more money into circulation.

about the shops, have they still got women running drill presses, etc.?*

By the way bud, do you ever see anything of Pat Sirdevan? I havent heard from him in two months. Well, its pretty near time for retreat so will close.

With loads of love for all
Fred
Bugler F.A. Kittleman
Btry F. 304th F.A.
Amex Forces

◆ ◆ ◆

March 4 1919
Ferce France

Dear brother,

Your letter of Feb 11 received, and was very glad to hear from you. A little advice before I continue. If I were you I would write

---

*Like many soldiers, Fred was curious about the women throughout the country who had taken factory jobs while so many men were fighting abroad. He may also have worried about whether these women would return to their household chores once men returned to reclaim their old jobs. The fears harbored by many men were illusory. Only about one million women took jobs in war work, and relatively few of them were in heavy industry. Furthermore, most of these women left their jobs by 1919 and eventually married and had children. But their wartime service contributed at least modestly to the cause of women's rights—for example, with the ratification in 1920 of the 19th Amendment giving them the vote.[17]

all my letters on a typewriter, because I can make out every word, whereas, if you do a little pencil lashing I can only read half of it.

Its been raining for the last couple of day's, which makes it very disagreeable. I just came off from guard, a while ago and now have the rest of the day to myself.

You want the latest dope, when we sail for home? Well the date officially set has been fixed at April 10th.

Another thing, you asked me to bring home some souvenirs, well bud, I will do so if you send me a little "kale" to buy them. You know the little money I draw don't go a helluva ways. Its all I draw is (61) sixty-one francs a month, and out of this I have to pay for my washing (to lazy to do it myself) a few bottles of vin rouge, a little candy, and cigarettes & boom! Its all gone, in less than a week. You see its this way, you have to pay (5) five times as much as a thing is worth.

I have been sending home a few copies of the Stars & Stripes, which are very interesting. You have no doubt received some of them by now.

I havent heard from Geo Finger in over a month. I sure would be glad to see him go home, as he has been over here long enough.

One thing more before I close, what is the average pay the machinists are now making, while working day work?

Can't think of anything more to write so had better ring off.

> With loads of love
> Fred
> Bugler F.A. Kittleman
> Btry F. 304th F.A.
> Amex Forces
> France

◆ ◆ ◆

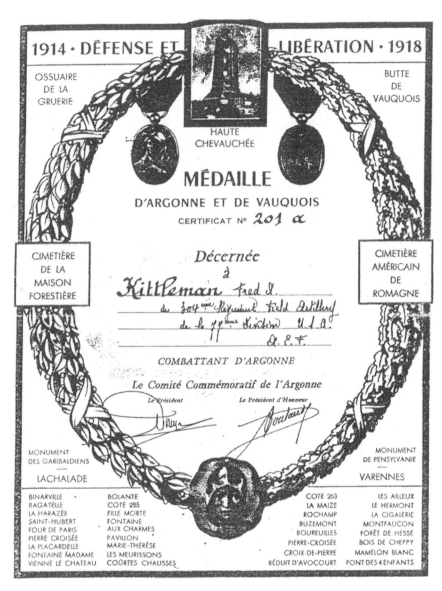

FIGURE 19. Fred's Citation from the French Government. Courtesy of Robert Deckman.

Sun. Mar 15 `9`9
Ferce, France

Dear Mother,

Received your letters of Feb 22nd and will now try to answer. These letters were the first I had received in pretty near three weeks, so I was beginning to worry, lest something had happened at home. You people must of put an awfull lot of faith in the junk which was printed in the "Olean Times" about the 77th sailing March 5th, but I don't think they will be out of the way over a month or more. There is a notice on our bulletin board stating that we will sail about April 1st for the good old U.S.A. So I think you can expect me home by the latter part of April, at the most.

This will probably be the last letter you will receive from France from me, so do not worry.

News is very scarce as its the same old game from one day to another, so I hardly know what to write about, except to tell about the weather, etc.

Before I forget I went to the 77th Div. Field meet at Parce yesterday. Will enclose the official organ of the 77th Div., "The Wash," so you will find out all about it. It's a very amusing paper. Will also send a copy of last weeks "Stars and Stripes" under separate cover.

I am well and OK and hope that this letter will find you all the same. Hoping to see you real soon.

Your loving son
Fred
Bugler F. A. Kittleman
Btry F. 304th F.A.
Amex Forces

Letters / 111

P.S. Give the neighbours my best wishes.

Finis

◆ ◆ ◆

With "Finis" Fred hoped that he would be writing no more letters from France. But departure for America would meet with further delays. He was still in Fercé when he wrote the following letter. He mentions cooties once again. These pests continued to be a problem for most soldiers. After the armistice everyone in Fred's battery was sent to a delousing station on more than one occasion.

◆ ◆ ◆

April 6 1919
Sunday

Dear brother,

Received your welcome letter of Mar 15th and was very glad to see that you still think of me.

You suggestion is a very good one in regards to pass forms, so am sending two, duly signed, the other one I gave to Jim Clancy, so he also can get a pass.* As soon as we get to New York, and I don't think it will be very long, I will wire you that I have arrived safely from overseas. You can then do the rest.

---

*Here it appears that Fred is referring to passes on the Pennsylvania Railroad. These would have permitted Harry and a friend to visit Fred upon his arrival in New York. There is no evidence that Harry managed to make that trip.

We received the needle last Thursday, a 3 in 1 shot, and some shot O ye gods, but my arm was sore. And tomorrow, Monday, is our formal inspection, called the Embarkation inspection. Every man must have full equipment, be free from cooties and venereal diseases, or else he is liable to stay over here for some time.

The latest dope I have is that we sail for the U.S. on about April 18th on the S.S. America. Pretty good stuff eh!

Now about that Liberty Cabbage and the 2 cases [of wine?] in the storm shed. I would like to get at it for about an hour. It would be "finie."

Received a letter from George F[inger] yesterday together with his picture. He doesnt seem to have changed a bit.

Well bud will have to ring off.

> Love to all,
> Fred
> Bugler F.A. Kittleman
> Btry F. 304th F.A.
> Amex Forces

◆ ◆ ◆

The following was the last letter Fred wrote to his family. Even this one had to be read and signed by one of the battery's lieutenants. For once, his information regarding departure for America was (almost) correct. Shortly before this letter was written, the men in Battery F had marched from Fercé to the nearby village of La Suze, where they joined other units from the 304th Field Artillery. There they had their final delousings, drills, and inspections. On April 17 they boarded trains and arrived in Brest on the 18th.

FIGURE 20. Fred's Bugle. Courtesy of Robert Deckman.

◆ ◆ ◆

April 11 1919

Dear Mother,

Have a few spare moments, so will write a few lines to let you know I am kicking just as much as ever.

I wrote you a couple of weeks ago, which I thought would be my last letter but alas I was wrong. Nevertheless, I feel quiet confident that it wont be so very long before I am sailing for the good old U.S.A. The latest dope, this I think is official, is that we leave La Suze for Brest the 18th of April. We will in all probability remain at Brest for (4) four or (5) five days, possibly a week, and then adieu, Republic Francaise. We will parte L'Amerique toot sweet.*

I can picture the scene, when the men of the 77th Division, first catch sight of the statue of Liberty. (This is also our divisional shoulder insignia.) Gee but it makes me happy just thinking about it. You know I have been in France darn near a year, lacking about (3) weeks, so I have had, using a little slang, a belly full.

Well little mother will close for now hoping to see you all real soon.

Your loving son
Fred

Love to Helen & Harry

◆ ◆ ◆

In Brest there was yet one final set of delousings and inspections. The Army wanted the men to be clean and looking sharp when they arrived back in the states. On April 20, Easter Sunday, all the men in the 304th boarded the USS *Agamemnon*. It was a fitting irony

---

*Fred's jocular version of partir pour l'Amérique tout de suite—that is, leave for America right away.

FIGURE 21. Troops Arriving at Hoboken from France on the USS *Agamemnon*. Reprinted from *American Armies and Battlefields in Europe*.

that a German ship had brought them to France, and a German ship took them home. Before the United States seized it in 1917, the *Agamemnon* had been the *Kaiser Wilhelm II*, one of Germany's swiftest passenger steamers. Smaller than the *Leviathan*, the *Agamemnon* carried about 5,000 soldiers on this trip—the 304th, 305th, and 306th regiments plus sundry other small units and hundreds of wounded men. On April 29 the ship docked in Hoboken, and the men were then taken to Camp Mills on Long Island. Once in barracks there they were deloused yet again—the army's official name was "sanitation process." Then those men who wanted passes to visit New York City were allowed to go there. One can only assume that Fred was one of them. Although everyone was eager to return to civilian life, that would be delayed for several days.

The 77th Division had been the first division of draftees to make it to the front lines in France. There it established an enviable record.

As most of the 30,000 men who had served in the 77th at one time or another were from New York City, it had come to be known as "New York's Own." On May 5 the entire division arrived in the City in preparation for a grand parade. On that day's front page, the *New York Times* trumpeted the return of the gallant heroes:

> The 77th Division arrived in New York yesterday and became the guests of townsfolk whose hearts they long ago captured. When the first unit stepped ashore at the Thirty-fourth Street Ferry shortly after 10 o'clock in the morning the city capitulated to the friendly invasion long awaited. Throughout the afternoon and evening the appearance of the soldiers around the armories, where they are quartered, or on Broadway, was the signal for cheering that expressed New York's emotion.
>
> New York has declared this a holiday in honor of the heroes of the Argonne Forest. The schools will be closed to give the children an opportunity of viewing the parade, which will be a memorable military spectacle. Previous crowd records of the city will be broken, according to the police, when the multitudes gather along Fifth Avenue to see the division pass by.
>
> It was a gay scene at the Hotel Astor where the hob-nailed shoe of the enlisted man, the heavy boot of the officer, and the light dancing slippers of the girls beat rhythmic accompaniment to the music of several orchestras. The contrast to other scenes in the recent history of the division was so great that many of the men could do little more than sit up and wonder if it was all a dream.

Following the next day's glorious parade, the entire division was dispatched to Camp Upton for demobilization. The 304th Field Artillery ceased to exist on May 10, 1919. Despite the constant rain pelting them, the joyous men thronged to the quartermaster's office. There they turned in their blankets. Like all the others, Fred was allowed to keep his uniform, helmet, and gas mask. He also kept his battered bugle, which today is a prized possession of one of his grandsons. All the enlisted men were given $60, which amounted to about two months' pay. Fred then rushed to the train station, which took him into Manhattan. From there he boarded the train that would take him home to Olean. The Olean newspapers recorded that he arrived home on May 12. Two dozen other Olean men who had served in the 77th Division arrived back at about the same time. On May 14 all of them were feted in a victory dance held in the Knights of Columbus clubhouse.

Epilogue

The Return to Civilian Life

Fred was 23 years old when he arrived home in May 1919, and he could consider himself fortunate. He was not among the 26 men of the 304th Field Artillery who lost their lives. Altogether about 117,000 American troops died in the war: 53,000 battle fatalities and 63,000 non-combat deaths (including 47,000 who succumbed from influenza or its accompanying pneumonia). Several of Fred's close friends were among the 60 fatalities from his hometown.[1] Despite these significant losses, the United States emerged less scathed from the war than did most other belligerent nations. Altogether 17 million died in the war (10 million combatants and 7 million civilians), with more than 20 million others wounded. Military deaths for Russia totaled 1,700,000; for Britain and its empire, 908,000; for France, 1,357,000; for Germany, 1,773,000; for Austria-Hungary, 1,200,000. Tens of thousands of American and European soldiers who returned home were scarred psychologically or physically. Many suffered from shell shock (today called post-traumatic stress disorder). Others suffered from depression or disillusionment, as they wondered if all the bloodshed had been worth the cost. Writers like Ernest Hemingway, Gertrude Stein, and T. S. Eliot came to call all these survivors "the lost generation" or "the hollow men."

Although cities across the United States jubilantly feted their returning soldiers, it did not take long for most Americans to start wondering if entering the war had accomplished anything. The Versailles Peace Settlement of 1919 left almost no one happy. To many in France and Britain, it was too lenient. To Germany and its allies, it seemed overly vindictive. Because of the frustrations created by the settlement, some historians today consider the two world wars as one war with a mere cease fire in between. Believing that its participation in the war and the subsequent peace negotiations had accomplished little, the United States retreated into its traditional isolationism in the 1920s.

If Fred ever voiced anger or irritation about having had to serve his country, there is no record of it. As far as we can know today, his buoyant personality and patriotism helped him to avoid despondency. In this regard, he was like a majority of his fellow soldiers. In 1919 several state governments sent detailed questionnaires to returning veterans, asking them about their wartime experiences. Historian Edward A. Gutiérrez examined thousands of the responses that these ex-doughboys submitted. He found that the vast majority of them agreed that "war is hell" but also were proud of what they accomplished in "doing their bit" for Uncle Sam.[2]

This is not to say that Fred was entirely pleased with how the Army treated him after the war. The fact that he had not been admitted to a hospital when he was gassed on October 28, 1918, was to cause him problems for the next several decades. Because he was not hospitalized at the time, he was never inscribed in the official list of wounded soldiers. More than three months later, in February 1919, he was hospitalized, but the official reason was influenza. That illness was unfortunate, but it did not count as a combat wound.

The collection of papers now possessed by Fred's grandson, Robert Deckman, contains dozens of letters and other documents from the 1920s to the 1940s, all dealing with Fred's claim that his wartime service, especially the poison gas and influenza, left him with permanent health problems. Over several decades Fred corresponded with the Veterans Administration, and he gained support from the American Legion and the Veterans of Foreign Wars. (Through the 1920s Fred dealt with the Veterans Bureau. In 1930 that office and others dealing with ex-service personnel were combined to form the Department of Veterans Affairs, more commonly called the Veterans Administration.) As early as 1919, back home in Olean, he sought medical attention with local physicians for blood poisoning and what he simply called "stomach trouble." He also asserted that his "articular rheumatism was caused by exposure to elements, wet clothing and sleeping on the ground." Finally, in numerous letters to the government, he maintained that he developed cholecystitis (inflammation of the gallbladder) and varicocele (similar to varicose veins, a varicocele is an enlargement of the veins in the scrotum) while in the service. He provided evidence that for many years he had to buy many boxes of "Dr. Rainey's tablets" for relief of his stomach aches.

After years of attempting to obtain some level of disability compensation, Fred finally received a favorable reply. In 1930 he was deemed to have 25 percent permanent disability, and the Veterans Administration started payments to him of $12.00 per month. These payments lasted until April 1933. The discontinuance of his monthly allotment was not a negative judgment on him personally. At that time most World War I veterans whose disabilities were not deemed permanent were removed from the rolls. The available documentation does not indicate why the government reversed its earlier decision and now decided that his disability was not permanent.

Even before the discontinuance, Fred continued to plead for a permanent service-related allowance. The October 1932 issue of *The Pirate Piece*, a newsletter published by the 304th Field Artillery's regimental association, published an open letter that Fred wrote to Rupert B. Thomas, Jr., a lieutenant in charge of the gun battery to which Fred had been assigned. Fred stated:

> If you will remember back in 1918, in October, about the 27th or 28th in our gun positions above Fleville, (Willis Dever and myself volunteered to dig in the No. 1 gun) the gun position was completed and you were setting guns for line of fire, when the Germans started to throw some of their iron rations, with gas for dessert. Dever received a good dose of gas and was evacuated to the hospital the next morning with a few more of F men. I did not get up for reveille that morning, feeling pretty tough and was detailed to the picket line for 3 days to manicure horses and other little incidentals that go along with the job, all the while not feeling good, and afraid to say anything lest I get more details [that is, fearing that if he complained all that would happen is that he'd be given more work]. When the Nov. 1st drive started, [I] was sent back to the guns, which had been moved back to another position.
>
> Since I have been discharged, I have been having considerable trouble with my stomach, and the doctors seem inclined to think that the cause is gas. I've doctored since 1920 and intend to secure affidavits from the physicians who have attended me. . . . [S]o, Lieutenant, if you can do anything for me, [I] will appreciate the favor very much.

The 304th F.A.'s newsletter, *The Pirate Piece*, got its fanciful title from the nickname given to a piece of field artillery that was detached from its battery and sent forward to the infantry lines with orders to fire at short range, often in direct view of the enemy. Even in his letter on such a serious topic, Fred showed that he also had retained his sense of humor. Manicuring horses was his way of describing trimming their hooves. Various military veterans who knew Fred endeavored to plead his case. In July 1933, for example, T. A. Eaton, an officer in Olean's VFW barracks wrote to the Veterans Administration, noting that Fred had been gassed twice, the time of October 28, 1918, being the worst. But, Eaton states, "like many others, he did not report to a Field Dressing Station. In fact, it was necessary that those who were at all able to stand on their feet, to remain and man the guns and allow the most serious cases to go back for treatment. Due to this there is naturally no hospital record of this veteran being gassed. . . . This veteran did, nevertheless, enter a French Hospital with Influenza, during Feb. 1919, . . . but it is problematical whether there were ever any records kept in instances of this kind." Unflagging in his efforts to help Fred, Eaton wrote another letter, in November 1934, stating "he is one of those who were gassed but has no hospital record to that effect, as they were short of men to man the guns and he stuck and suffered rather than go to the rear." Moreover, several veterans from Battery F wrote affidavits affirming the truth of all that Fred claimed regarding gas attacks. Unfortunately for Fred, the fact that he did not receive medical attention immediately after being gassed meant that there was no paper trail to substantiate his claim that some of his health issues resulted from his wartime service. Over the next several years the Veterans Administration continued to deny his claims for continued partial disability allowance.

Fred was far from alone in believing that the government had not adequately thanked him for his wartime hardships. Thousands of other veterans failed to attain financial allotments for their injuries—though, admittedly, some of their claims about being gassed or shot probably were false or exaggerated. Moreover, many veterans argued that the government owed them bonuses as compensation for the income they lost while away from their regular employment back home.

In 1924 the government acceded to their demands and passed the World War Adjusted Compensation Act, which stipulated that every veteran would receive $1.00 for each day of domestic service and $1.25 for each day overseas. Each veteran was issued a certificate stating the amount he would receive. The only problem was that these certificates could not be redeemed until 1945. At that late date each veteran would be paid the face value plus interest. The reason for the 21-year delay was that the government did not have the funds to pay the veterans immediately. Thus a trust fund was to be created, with the government depositing money into it every year until 1945.

With the onset of the Great Depression in 1929, many veterans were out of work. They lobbied unsuccessfully for immediate payment of their certificates. Finally, in the spring and summer of 1932 some 17,000 veterans along with 25,000 family members and supporters marched on Washington, DC, and set up camp in a vacant, swampy area. They became known as the Bonus Army or Bonus Marchers. President Herbert Hoover refused to accede to their demands and ordered Army Chief of Staff General Douglas MacArthur to disperse them. Using infantry, cavalry, and tanks MacArthur swiftly drove the makeshift "army" out of town and burned all their belongings. A smaller bonus march arrived in the nation's capital the following year. Recently elected President Franklin Delano Roosevelt did not redeem the certificates, but he did offer jobs to many of the veterans in the newly created Civilian Conservation Corps, one of his New Deal programs designed to give jobs to the unemployed. In 1936 Congress overrode Roosevelt's veto and agreed to give veterans their bonuses nine years early.

Fred had not participated in the bonus marches. One reason was that he was fortunate in having a job. In a letter dated January 1, 1925, the Veterans Bureau had informed Fred that his Adjusted Service Certificate amounted to $1,189.00.[3] In the absence of any surviving records, one can assume that in 1936 Fred received that amount plus interest, for a total of about $1,200.00—in today's dollars, $15,600.00. In the midst of the Great Depression, that would have been a significant windfall for a working man with a young family to support.

It is impossible for us today to know whether Fred's lingering health problems were a direct result of his combat experiences. What can be stated with assurance is that Fred was no malingerer, fraud, or hypochondriac. He had performed bravely during his service at the Front. He was convinced that persistent stomach trouble and other problems resulted from his military service. He never claimed that he was totally disabled. All that he asked was some modest compensation for ailments that he had never had prior to the war but that bothered him from the time he was discharged to the end of his life.

Obviously, he was disappointed by the decisions of the Veterans Administration, but this did not make him cynical or unpatriotic. From the 1920s to his death in 1976, he was widely known as a friendly, happy man. The sense of humor evident in his wartime letters remained with him for the rest of his life. His grandchildren and other relatives and friends recall that he was a jokester right up to the end.

Fortunately for Fred, he was never without work after he returned home. The U.S. government had provided him with a certificate certifying that he had served in the military and asking employers to provide him with a satisfactory position. He never needed to use that document. Upon his return to Olean, he resumed his job at the Pennsylvania Railroad. There he earned 72 cents per hour. Over the next decade he held jobs as a machinist in other railroads and in factories. But the "prosperous" 1920s were not prosperous for him, for with every job he had to take a pay cut.

From 1924 to 1927 he and his cousin Bill Gabler tried their luck at operating a restaurant, but Fred estimated that he earned only $30 a week in that enterprise. Olean city directories of the mid-1920s list the business, known simply as "Gabler and Kittleman," and note that it served "soft drinks." Though officially a restaurant, this establishment was primarily a speakeasy. That was the era of Prohibition, which lasted from 1920 until its repeal in 1933. Fred and his cousin served alcoholic beverages, most likely in a back room. Given Fred's fondness for beer and wine, as seen in his wartime letters, one can be sure that he was no fan of Prohibition. His ledger from that business survives and is stored with his letters in the St. Bonaventure University archives. That book shows that 161 customers were allowed to run up bar tabs—that is, they could buy on credit. All of the names listed were those of men, with no women or families mentioned. Two of the men were simply listed as Big Mike and Leo of the "sewer gang." Fred's grandson Robert Deckman recalls his family joking about how Fred's speakeasy obtained its bathtub gin from a farm a couple of miles away.

The ability of Fred and his cousin to operate a bar with little fear of trouble from the authorities is understandable, given what is known about Olean in this period. The city was located on one of the busiest bootlegging routes between Chicago and New York City. It earned the nickname "Little Chicago," because Al Capone and other big-city gangsters often spent days or weeks at a time there. Olean provided a safe haven when such characters needed some time away from rival gangs or from the police back home. The Olean police were known to close their eyes to the shady activities of these notorious visitors as long as they caused no problems during their stays in town.

The chief of police in those years was Jack Dempsey (no relation to the boxer). Dempsey himself was well known as a bootlegger and as the organizer of cock fights in back of his home. Fred's tavern was so respectable that one of its regular bar customers was Father Williams of the nearby Catholic parish.

In the end, Fred and his cousin proved to be too generous for their own good. Dozens of customers never paid what they owed, and so Fred was forced to write "no more" or "no good" under their names and stop serving them. The ledger shows that when Fred and his cousin gave up the business late in 1927 dozens of people still owed what amounted to hundreds of dollars.

FIGURE 22. Fred's mother Josephine, Fred, and daughter Rita, 1920. Courtesy of Lois Zach.

Shortly thereafter Fred returned to work as a machinist, but that job paid only 55 cents per hour. In 1931 he obtained a position as general laborer in the Olean post office, where he earned $20 per week. In the midst of the Great Depression, he was perhaps lucky to have any kind of employment at all. We know about Fred's income in these years because he had to list his jobs in the forms he filled out in his efforts to obtain a modest disability allowance from the government.[4]

FIGURE 23. Lucinda and Fred, ca. 1946. Courtesy of Donna Kayes.

His meager income would have made life difficult even if Fred had remained single. But in the 1920s he became a family man. Soon after his return to Olean he met Lucinda Wilson, and the two of them were married early in 1920. They moved to a house just a few blocks from where Fred had grown up. By 1924 Fred and Lucinda had three daughters, Rita, Harriet, and Helen. In addition, Fred's mother Josephine had moved in with them and would remain a member of the household until her death in 1937. She passed away on what should have been a happy day: her 63rd birthday.

Fred's brother Harry died on August 4, 1920, at the age of 22. He had never married. On the same day he passed away, his obituary in the local papers noted that he had been ill for months but did not list the cause of death. Evidently Harry was just as sociable as his brother Fred. The *Olean Evening Times* noted that Harry had been "one of the best known young men in the city [and] . . . was very popular among the young people." Fred's sister Helen married Olean man Rudolph Wenke in 1924. They lived most of their life together in and around Buffalo. She remained an avid piano player throughout the decades, which undoubtedly pleased her mother Josephine and brother Fred. Music was a big part of the family. Two of Josephine's brothers were among the most prominent band leaders and musicians in western New York through the first half of the century.

By all accounts Fred was a loving and hard-working husband and father and one who never complained about his limited resources. Most of his friends started calling him "Fritz." The family's finances finally took a turn for the better in the early 1930s, when Fred was promoted to letter carrier in the post office. He held that job until 1954, when problems with his legs forced him to retire.

Throughout his life he remained an unflinching patriot. On December 8, 1941, the day after the Japanese attack on Pearl Harbor, he went to the naval recruiting office in Olean and tried to enlist. He was 45 years old at that time. The recruiter called him an old man and sent him away. It should be stressed that he tried to join the navy, not the army. In 1965 Fred's grandson, Robert Deckman, was fresh out of high school and planning to join some branch of the armed forces. Fred urged him to join the navy, because he did not want the young man to go through what he himself had endured fighting on land in World War I. His grandson took that advice. Fred's loyalty to Uncle Sam was further demonstrated by his lifelong membership in the Olean post of the Veterans of Foreign Wars; at various times he held different offices, including one stint as commander. In 1961 he attended the national convention of the Veterans of World War I in Dallas, Texas. The medal that he wore when attending that event is now part of the collection of his letters in the Friedsam Memorial Library.

The final decades of Fred's life were generally happy ones. He liked to draw, collect coins, and repair mechanical devices. He was an active member of his Catholic parish as well as the local Eagles Club. He and his wife Lucinda were devoted parents and grandparents. After Lucinda died in 1968, Fred spent even more time with his grandchildren, telling them stories and taking them fishing. His granddaughter Beverly Hollander recalls that Fred kept his old bugle prominently displayed on a wall. Frequently he took it down and regaled his family with a variety of tunes. He also played a harmonica. His adoring grandchildren affectionately called him "Poppie."

Fred passed away on August 11, 1976, and was buried near his wife, his mother, his brother, and other relatives in the St. Bonaventure Cemetery just outside Olean. He had been an "ordinary" man. But his kindness, his conviviality, his love of family and friends, his bravery, and his devotion to his country marked him as extraordinary.

Notes

Introduction

1. Adam Hochschild, in *New York Times Book Review*, May 18, 2014, 16.

2. The following are excellent recent accounts on the origins of the war: Christopher Clark, *The Sleepwalkers: How Europe Went to War in 1914* (New York: Harper, 2013); Max Hastings, *Catastrophe 1914: Europe Goes to War* (New York: Knopf, 2013); Sean McMeekin, *July 1914: Countdown to War* (New York: Basic Books, 2013).

3. On the general conduct of the war see the works cited in the Suggested Readings plus the following: Mark Adkin, *The Western Front Companion: The Complete Guide to How the Armies Fought for Four Devastating Years 1914–1918* (London: Aurum, 2013); Hans Ehlert, Michael Epkenhans, Gerhard P. Gross, eds., *The Schlieffen Plan: International Perspectives on the German Strategy for World War I*. English trans. edited by David T. Zabecki (Lexington: University Press of Kentucky, 2014).

4. Quoted by Harold Evans, *New York Times Book Review*, May 12, 2013, 1.

5. On this entire affair see Erik Larson, *Dead Wake: The Last Crossing of the Lusitania* (New York: Broadstreet Books, 2015).

6. On submarine warfare and the Zimmermann telegram see, among other works: Jay Winter, ed., *The Cambridge History of the First World War* (New York: Cambridge University Press, 2014), I: 40, 79–80, 115–16, 154–55,

337–39, 525–32, and passim; Lawrence Sondhaus, *The Great War at Sea: A Naval History of the First World War* (New York: Cambridge University Press, 2014); Thomas Boghardt, *The Zimmermann Telegram: Intelligence, Diplomacy, and America's Entry into World War I* (Annapolis, MD: Naval Institute Press, 2012).

7. Olean City Directories for 1916–1918; Harry's obituary of August 4, 1920, in the *Olean Evening Herald* and the *Olean Evening Times.*

8. "65 Drafted Men Leave," *Olean Evening Times*, February 20, 1918; also articles in the *Olean Evening Herald:* "Schedule for Sendoff," February 20, 1918, and "Final Arrangements," February 22, 1918.

Letters

1. Winter, *The Cambridge History of the First World War,* I: 512–17.

2. *Olean Evening Times,* July 6, 1917.

3. On this and other points see Edward M. Coffman, *The War to End All Wars: The American Military Experience in World War I* (New York, 1968), 65 and passim.

4. *Olean Evening Herald:* January 3, 1918 ("Olean to Be Dark") and January 18, 1918 (letter from State Fuel Administrator).

5. Paul E. Fontenoy, "Convoy System," in Spencer C. Tucker, ed., *The Encyclopedia of World War I: A Political, Social and Military History* (Santa Barbara, CA: ABC-CLIO, 2005), I: 312–14.

6. Heather Jones, "Prisoners of War," http://www.bl.uk/world-war-one/articles/prisoners-of-war.

7. Howard, *Autobiography of a Regiment,* 57.

8. The most detailed work on this topic is Xu Guiqu, *Strangers on the Western Front: Chinese Workers in the Great War* (Cambridge, MA: Harvard University Press, 2011); also see Rebecca Karl's review of that book in the *London Review of Books* (December 1, 2011), 23–24.

9. For an excellent account of a French artillery unit, which operated in similar fashion, see Martha Hanna, *Your Death Would Be Mine: Paul and*

Marie Pireaud in the Great War (Cambridge, MA: Harvard University Press, 2006), 82–85, 92–94, and passim.

10. Quoted by David J. Jackowe, www.historynet.com/poison-gas-comes-to-america.htm.

11. See Marek Pruszewicz, "How Deadly Was the Poison Gas of WWI," www.bbc.com/news/magazine-31042472; "Poison Gas," http://spartacus-educational.com/FWWgas.htm; Charles E. Heller, *Chemical Warfare in World War I: The American Experience, 1917–1918*, Leavenworth Papers No. 10 (Fort Leavenworth, KS: U.S. Army Command and General Staff College, 1984).

12. Reprinted in *Olean Evening Herald*, November 21, 1918.

13. Cameramen in the signal corps caught some of this on film: https://www.youtube.com/watch?v'GmFQr-M5GQU; https://www.youtube.com/watch?v'A1qceHiQX_I.

14. See *Olean Evening Times*, December 26, 1918. This event was filmed and parts can be seen on YouTube: https://www.youtube.com/watch?v'xjXFk-nwL9U.

15. https://www.youtube.com/watch?v'-BXg16pe_sI; https://www.youtube.com/watch?v'btpA77X7pCI; https://www.youtube.com/watch?v'f5fKs0dkQq4.

16. 1934 affidavit in the Robert Deckman papers.

17. See David M. Kennedy, *Over Here: The First World War and American Society* (New York: Oxford University Press, 1980), 284–87; Carrie Brown, *Rosie's Mom: Forgotten Women Workers of the First World War* (Boston: Northeastern University Press, 2002).

Epilogue

1. American War and Military Operations Casualties: Lists and Statistics, https://fas.org/sgp/crs/natsec/RL32492.pdf; "91 from Cattaraugus County," *Olean Evening Herald*, October 14, 1922.

2. Gutiérrez, *Doughboys on the Great War: How American Soldiers Viewed Their Military Service* (Lawrence: University Press of Kansas, 2014).

3. This letter and numerous others on related topics are in the collection of papers in the possession of Fred's grandson, Robert Deckman.

4. Copies of the forms are in the Deckman papers.

Suggested Readings

There are thousands of books and articles on World War I, and the list has grown exponentially with the new works that have appeared to commemorate the centenary of that conflict. The items listed below are simply a guide to some of the best or most relevant books dealing with the topic.

On the 77th Division

American Battle Monuments Commission. *77th Division: Summary of Operations in the World War.* Washington, DC: U.S. Government Printing Office, 1944.

Gaff, Alan D. *Blood in the Argonne: The "Lost Battalion" of World War I.* Norman: University of Oklahoma Press, 2005.

Glass, Joseph, Henry L. Miller, and Osmund O'Brien. *The Story of Battery D, 304th Field Artillery. September 1917 to May 1919.* New York: privately printed, 1919 (reprint by Nabu Press in 2010).

Howard, James M. *The Autobiography of a Regiment: A History of the 304th Field Artillery in the World War.* New York: privately printed, 1920.

McKeogh, Arthur. *The Victorious 77th Division (New York's Own) in the Argonne Fight.* New York: John H. Eggers Co., 1919.

United States Army, Infantry Division, 77th. *History of the Seventy-Seventh Division, August 25th, 1917, November 11th, 1918. Designed and Written in the Field, France.* New York: W. H. Crawford Company, 1919.

On Overall American Involvement in the War

American Battle Monuments Commission. *American Armies and Battlefields in Europe: A History, Guide, and Reference Book*. Washington, DC: U.S. Government Printing Office, 1938.

Clark, George B. *The American Expeditionary Force in World War I: A Statistical History 1917–1919*. Jefferson, NC: McFarland, 2013.

Coffman, Edward M. *The War to End All Wars: The American Experience in World War I*. New York: Oxford University Press, 1968.

Dalessandro, Robert J., and Rebecca S. Dalessandro. *Over There: America in the Great War*. Mechanicsburg, PA: Stackpole Books, 2016.

Farwell, Byron. *Over There: The United States in the Great War, 1917–1918*. New York: W. W. Norton, 2000.

Ferrell, Robert H. *America's Deadliest Battle: Meuse-Argonne, 1918*. Lawrence: University Press of Kansas, 2007.

Fletcher, Arthur Lloyd. *History of the 113th Field Artillery 30th Division*. Raleigh, NC: The History Committee of the 113th F.A., 1920.

Gutiérrez, Edward A. *Doughboys on the Great War: How American Soldiers Viewed Their Military Service*. Lawrence: University Press of Kansas, 2014.

Keene, Jennifer D. *World War I: The American Soldier Experience*. Lincoln: University of Nebraska Press, 2011.

Kingsbury, Celia M. *For Home and Country: World War I Propaganda on the Home Front*. Lincoln: University of Nebraska Press, 2010.

Lengel, Edward G. *Thunder and Flames: Americans in the Crucible of Combat, 1917–1918*. Lawrence: University Press of Kansas, 2015.

Woodward, David. *The American Army and the First World War*. New York: Cambridge University Press, 2014.

On the War in General

Clark, Christopher. *The Sleepwalkers: How Europe Went to War in 1914*. New York: Harper, 2013.

Englund, Peter. *The Beauty and the Sorrow: An Intimate History of the First World War*. New York: Knopf, 2011.

Fletcher, Anthony. *Life, Death, and Growing Up on the Western Front*. New Haven, CT: Yale University Press, 2013.

Hastings, Max. *Catastrophe 1914: Europe Goes to War*. New York: Knopf, 2013.

Holborn, Mark, and Hilary Roberts, *The Great War: A Photographic Narrative*. New York: Knopf, 2013.

Lengel, Edward G., ed. *A Companion to the Meuse-Argonne Campaign*. Maldon, MA: Wiley Blackwell, 2014.

Mayhew, Emily. *Wounded: A New History of the Western Front*. New York: Oxford University Press, 2013.

Preston, Diana. *A Higher Form of Killing: Six Weeks in World War I That Forever Changed the Nature of Warfare*. London: Bloomsbury, 2015.

Storey, William Kelleher. *The First World War: A Concise Global History*. Lanham, MD: Rowman & Littlefield, 2009.

Strachan, Hew. *The First World War*. New York: Viking, 2004.

Tucker, Spencer C., ed. *World War I: The Definitive Encyclopedia and Document Collection*. Santa Barbara: ABC-Clio, 2014.

Winter, Jay, ed. *The Cambridge History of the First World War*. 3 volumes. New York: Cambridge University Press, 2014.

Index

Agamemnon, 115–16

Argonne, *see* Meuse-Argonne

Army, United States, size, xviii, 9;
304th Field Artillery, xxiii, 5–6,
28, 49–51, 58–59, 68, 76, 83, 84,
91, 94–95, 97, 116; 77ᵗʰ Division,
1–2, 6, 49–51, 58, 62, 91, 107,
111, 116–18; lack of preparation,
21–22, 38; total fatalities, 119

Aubepierre-sur-Aube, 85

Baccarat sector, 49–50, 53, 58, 88

Berlin, Irving, 2

Bogart, Humphrey, 24

Bonaparte, Napoleon, 26

Bonus Army, 124

Bordeaux, 27, 45–46

Brest, 26, 114, 115

Briquenay, 84

Camp de Souge, 27, 33, 36, 46

Camp Mills, 116

Camp Upton, 1–3, 8–10, 21, 118

Capone, Al, 126

Christopher, Fred, 103

Censorship of letters, 24, 61, 77, 85

Chinese workers, 37–38

Clarke, John P., 82

Cohan, George M., 34

Deckman, Robert, 126, 130

Dempsey, Jack, 127

Dever, Willis, 82, 122

Dozol, Eliza, 102

Dubler, Ernest, 77

Eaton, T.A., 123

Edel, Xavier, 39, 41, 59, 66, 78

Fagan. Albert, 72

Fercé, 97–98

Finger, Ed, 55, 78

Finger, George, 33, 55, 109

Fismes, 53, 58, 133

Four de Paris, 76

Franz Josef, xii

Franz Ferdinand, xii

French people, 32, 35, 60, 87

French 75mm Field Gun, 28, 29, 67

Gabler, Christie, 73
Gabler, Donina, 19
Gabler, "Red," 67
Gabler, William, 126

Hague Conference, 63
Hartweg, Louis, 56, 61
Harty, Herman, 21
Harvey, Ambrose, 59, 86, 96
Hollander, Beverly, 130
Hoover, Herbert, 124
Hurd, Charles, 66

Inoculations, 12–14, 17, 113

Jordan, Frank R., 80–81

Kittleman, Frederick Albert, armistice, 84, 89; bugle, 34, 35, 38, 40; clothing and food, 10–11; departure for army, xx; departure from France, 111–16; drinking, 34–35, 36, 53, 56, 94, 126–27; early life, xviii–xix; employment history, 125–27, 129; health problems and government payments, 120–24; inoculations, 12–14, 17, 113; last years, 129–30; life insurance, 19; patriotism, 32, 43, 46–47, 61, 129–30; poison gas, 63, 82–83; religion, 15, 57, 73–74, 104; return home, 118; Spanish flu, 100–01; training, 20; wages, 40, 54, 57, 66, 71, 109; war deaths and destruction, 54, 58–59, 62–63, 72, 74, 88; women, 18–19, 26, 32, 39, 42, 43–44, 48, 56, 72, 73, 75, 94

Kittleman, Frederick Alfred, xix, 39, 52, 74, 75
Kittleman, Harry, xix, 5, 21, 23, 56–57, 60, 71, 72, 77, 96, 129
Kittleman, Helen (Wenke), xix, 16, 41–42, 45, 55, 66, 71, 78–79, 93, 96, 104–06, 129
Kittleman, Harriet (Chambers), 129
Kittleman, Helen (Deckman, Fred's daughter), 129
Kittleman, Josephine, xix, 39, 74, 129
Kittleman, Lucinda (Wilson), 129, 130
Kittleman, Rita (Hollander), 129
Knights of Columbus, xx, 81, 118
Koenig, Peter, 100

Lasky movie, 12, 15
Leviathan, 24, 27
Lice, 23, 52, 55, 76–77, 79, 90–91, 112, 115
Lusitania, xvii

MacArthur, Douglas, 124

Mahan, A. T., 63
Matter, William C., 82
McManus, James, 82, 86
Meuse-Argonne, 68–70, 81–83, 87–88
Moore, Charlie, 22
Moore, "Dot," 18

National Guard, xviii, 47
Nicholas II, xiii
Nobles, Louie, 43, 44

Oise-Aisne sector, 58, 61, 88
Olean, xix–xx, 15–16, 46, 73, 126–27

Pattituce, Nino, 52
Pennsylvania Railroad, xix, 5, 60, 125
Pershing, John J., xviii, 69, 91, 107
poison gas, 63–65, 82–83
Princip, Gavrilo, xii
Prisoners of war, 28–29, 30
Prohibition, 126–27

Red Cross, 15–16, 81
Rockefeller, John D., xix
Roosevelt, Franklin Delano, 124

Schlieffen Plan, xv
Sirdevan, Ester, 56
Sirdevan, Pat, 56, 108
Spanish flu, 100–01, 107

Stars and Stripes, 97
Studholme, Foster, 7, 56

Thomas, Rupert B., Jr., 122
Truman, Harry S., 69

United States, aftermath of the war, 119–20; neutrality, xv–xvi, 7; patriotism, 29–30

Versailles Peace Settlement, 120
Veterans Administration, 121–25
Vesle sector, 53–54, 58, 88

Wenke, Rudolph, 129
Wenke, Otto, 71
Whitman, Charles, 8
Wilhelm II, xii, xvii
Wilson, Margaret, 15
Wilson, Woodrow, xv–xvi, xvii, 8, 91
Women in the workforce, 54–55, 108
World War, First, armistice, 83, 89; German offensives, 28 origins; xi–xiv; submarines, xvi–xviii, 24–25, 30
World War Adjusted Compensation Act, 124–25

Y.M.C.A., 12–13, 15
York, Alvin C., 68

Zimmermann telegram, xviii

Made in the USA
Lexington, KY
21 February 2017